GARLAND STUDIES ON

THE ELDERLY IN AMERICA

edited by

STUART BRUCHEY
UNIVERSITY OF MAINE

A GARLAND SERIES

DECODING THE CULTURAL STEREOTYPES ABOUT AGING

NEW PERSPECTIVES ON AGING TALK AND AGING ISSUES

EVELYN M. O'REILLY

GARLAND PUBLISHING, INC.
NEW YORK & LONDON / 1997

Library of Congress Cataloging-in-Publication Data

O'Reilly, Evelyn M., 1931–
    Decoding the cultural stereotypes about aging : new perspec-
tives on aging talk and aging issues / Evelyn M. O'Reilly.
        p.   cm. — (Garland studies on the elderly in America)
    Includes bibliographical references and index.
    ISBN 0-8153-3023-5 (alk. paper)
    1. Aged—Psychology. 2. Aged—Attitudes. 3. Stereotype
(Psychology) 4. Old age—Public opinion. 5. Aging in literature.
I. Title. II. Series.
HQ1061.074 1997
305.26'0973—dc21   97-33172

Printed on acid-free, 250-year-life paper
Manufactured in the United States of America

This book is dedicated to my daughter Sharon,
as she cherishes her gift from heaven.

Contents

Foreword

Aging has always been a term that is prominent in our American culture. We encounter the term in the literature, the media, the market place, the health care system, and even the scam artist's repertoire. It is just a simple word, yet it connotes so many inferences.

Consider the concept of aging; can anyone truly define it? I will briefly try to trace its origin. Prior to the nineteenth century people talked about old age, but in a different context than discussions in the twentieth century. Americans identified stages of life; but actual demarcations between the stages to categorize people were not important. Age was not a significant marker in peoples lives.

However, by the end of the century, new advances in medicine identified variations in health patterns of individuals. Many of the deteriorating illnesses occurred during the later years of life, including cognitive impairment. Finally, the term "senile" emerged. This term was really a societal label for degenerating brain efficiency. Gradually, differences between lifespan stages began to evolve.

Eventually, age consciousness developed as "the new kid on the block." In most instances this process was a quiet positive evolution for individuals as they advanced in years. However, age stratification also emerged, and the concept of aging developed. What is this concept? Is it an enigma? When does it begin? It is from this background that this study evolved.

Sharon E. Naum, BS, MBA

Preface

This study focuses on the language of aging. Its premise is that aging is a label, a symbol and a myth of cultural stereotypes that is part of the conditions of growing old in American society. The impetus for the study began through my professional work as a nurse educator, and as a practicing nurse in the hospital and community. It occurred to me that age-grading was an ongoing event with the health care team. I thought critically about these phenomena; I wondered if the labels indirectly affected the health teams' image of the aging individual. I discussed the concept with my colleagues, and they acknowledged my concerns. Why was this theory disturbing? Because I believe that stratifying aging individuals in the health care setting could lead to inadequate assessment of the clients' needs. Additionally, as a society, it blunts our sensitivity to what is really going on with the individual.

To enhance the salience of my hypothesis, I went into the community and listened to people talk about the aging individual. I solicited feedback from my relatives and friends. I asked colleagues in distant states to tape some conversations on aging for me. I visited a Caribbean island and observed people and talked to them during their normal everyday routines. A nurse colleague provided me with a taped conversation on the topic from the Irish countryside. As I decoded the language of aging, I wondered, was it a cultural construct? Did people reflectively view all aging individuals in a similar pattern, or was aging talk one thread in a skein of issues?

I searched the literature and discovered a wealth of information about the elderly and the aging individual. However, the search produced comparatively few studies on "The Language of Aging" which was the focus of my study.

Several forms of inquiry were used to implement the study, including viewing the media to identify the common themes of aging, participant observation and interviews of aging individuals and others in their homes and various locations. Data collection took place over eighteen months. Analysis was conducted from a structuralism framework.

Does aging occur at a precise time, and in precise categories, or through a shift in behavior? Travel with me through the chapters of this book, through the literature review, the settings where I interviewed the informants, the analysis, the patterns I discovered. Did the informants fit the stereotypes? Is the myth of aging just that--a myth?

This book offers all of us a chance to step outside our reflexive cultural backgrounds, if only for a brief period, to comprehend the world from the perspective of aging individuals who live each day with the myths and stereotypes of their cohort.

Acknowledgments

This book was inspired by my deceased parents, and my three children: Michael, Anne Marie and Sharon and their spouses; my six grand-daughters, and of course little Alexander Ryan; enriched by the previous contributions of my informants, my colleagues, many aging individuals, my students and friends; encouraged by the efforts of Assistant Editor Tania Bissell; Updated and revised through the continued, tireless support, of my daughter Sharon. To her a special thanks; and to her husband Chris. Finally, to the most important person in my life, my husband; who has sustained me in all my endeavors; Thanks Joe!

Decoding the Cultural Stereotypes about Aging

I

Introduction

I had just returned from a workshop titled Creative Aging. As I walked to my car, I reflected on the content of the program. Most vivid in my memory were the elderly participants: Mr. J., ninety-two years, who continues to work each day as a hospital volunteer; Mr. M., eighty-seven years, a recent widower who had to leave early to baby-sit for his grandchildren; Mrs. L., ninety years, who spoke about the voluntary committees she works on, as she coyly folded her cane-chair, least anyone notice she needed supportive assistance. The workshop had many interesting presentations, and yet these energetic individuals 'stole the show.'

What was different about these elderly individuals? Was it their enthusiasm or their energy? Were they unique and were their experiences irrelevant to myths about Aging? How can we know a person from the myth? How can we know the elderly from society's version of a category called Aging? To answer these questions, I looked at people talking about age-related matters. The premise of this study is that Aging is a label, a symbol or a set of myths which is part of the conditions of growing old in American Society. One of the main goals is to identify the markers that demarcate the boundaries of aging.

The study looks at aging in the media and other areas, in particular five selected settings in the community. The research addresses the following questions: What are the properties of this myth? When does the myth create tension? How are these tensions expressed?

Because older people are part of society, their behavior mirrors its attitudes and expectations. There are good reasons to say that since the advent of the Industrial Revolution, the aging population has been viewed quite negatively. Some symptoms of this are what many call a youth oriented society. Aging is viewed as unattractive, asexual, unemployable, and helpless. Even older people themselves may have inaccurate views of aging. Common beliefs are that old people are forgetful, dependent, frugal, paranoid, lazy, and so on. I believe these conceptions grossly exaggerate the actual facts, but they are important and must be studied carefully. By studying conceptions, rather than behaviors, this study explores questions not typically addressed by people who study aging. Many previous studies have identified behaviors, and quantified various aspects of the lives of the elderly. There are comparatively few studies of Aging as a cultural construct and this is what I try to remedy here.

In addressing myself to the reader I hope I have elucidated the notion that this research addresses the myth of Aging, not the many pseudo synonyms of aging that may be used throughout the study to refer to chronological age. It was difficult initially to organize this concept, and I hope the distinction is succinctly communicated.

REASONS FOR THE STUDY

My interest in this study evolved from my professional encounters with clients in the hospital and the community. As a nurse educator who works with students in giving care to aging people, I noticed that many members of the health team talked about these people in ways that did not always appear grounded in direct experience. I discussed this with other health care professionals who concurred with my premise.

When I explored this issue in the community I discovered a similar response. It was apparent to me that references to the elderly were addressed in a categorical manner. However, it became apparent that the labels assigned by nurses, physicians, and other members of the health team are different than those used by the lay community. For example, people in the community talk about the frail elderly, the gray panthers, the senior citizens, the old folks. There is a lot of emphasis placed on discounts for senior citizens, lunch programs, and outings for seniors. Many people qualify for these programs and avail themselves of the advantages.

In comparison, health team members use a biopsychosocial terminology which assumes that aging is a generalized biological deterioration throughout the body. These changes include a decrease in physiological function, that is: breathing, cardio-vascular capacity, bowel and bladder function, muscle strength, cartilage, and bone deterioration. In addition, many cognitive deficiencies are immediately relegated to the aging process, such as disorientation, or the inability to respond to institutional routines.

This raises concerns, as to the aging individual's capacity to adapt to his or her changing internal body conditions. Many physical complaints are glossed over by the physician and attributed to aging. The concern for safety in ambulation raises the questions, can the person live alone? Does she need to live in a nursing home? In many instances the decision is made by the health team. The patient and significant other are orchestrated into believing it is the best solution. I wondered if this reflexive type of approach influenced the patient's response to care, or the care-givers approach vis-a-vis the patient.

Perhaps the following stories will convey a more vivid picture of my thesis. The first story pertains to a 79 year-old woman, hospitalized for Paget's disease (a bone disease). She had fallen at home and sustained minor injuries. Prior to her hospitalization she had lived alone and maintained her own apartment with the assistance of a home health aide. A series of diagnostic tests revealed she had no injuries.

A discharge plan was initiated, and it was decided by the health team that it was not safe for her to live alone. Instead she needed to live in a nursing home. This was communicated to the patient's daughter and the patient, respectively. The patient objected bitterly, exclaiming, "I functioned sufficiently at home prior to my hospitalization, I can take care of myself!" The patient finally negotiated a successful outcome and returned home to her former life-style. Her daughter agreed to act as a support system. I believe this story depicts the sorting of people into categories according to an age-grade pattern.

While I recognize that some people do suffer illnesses of mind and body as a result of their age, individuals do differ. Frequently, people are categorized into age groups without individual assessment of the participant.

According to the literature, the increasing life expectancy of individuals is having a significant effect on aging adults, their families, significant others and the health care system. McCabe, Fulk and Staab report that the "older population is essentially a healthy one; more than half of the people over sixty-five years old are free of functional limitations," (p. 19) and many of this age group live independently in the community. For those who do require assistance, the informal network of family and friends is a viable resource. Consider the following demographic numbers:

> In 1995, the population of persons sixty-five years or older numbered 33.5 million. This represents 12.8 percent of the American population or an increase of 2.3 million people since 1990. Conversely, in 1900, there were 3.1 million people over sixty-five. (Administration on Aging:1996, Aging Into the 21st Century, p. 1-2)

> In 1995, the age cohort of people 65-74 years (18.8 million people), this reflects a population that was eight times Greater than 1900. The age cohort of people from 75-84 years (11.1 million people), this reflects a population that was fourteen times Greater than 1900. The age cohort from 85 years and older (3.6 million people), this reflects a population that was twenty-nine times greater than 1900. (Administration on Aging:1996, A Profile of Older Americans, p. 2)

Life Expectancy

The life expectancy of a male age 65 in 1995 was 15.6 years. The life expectancy of a female age 65 in 1995 was 18.9 years. A child born in 1995 could expect to live 75.8 years. Anticipated growth for the population age 65 or older is:

    1995 - 33.5 million people
    2010 - 39.4 million people
    2030 - 69.0 million people
    2050 - 79.0 million people

(Administration on Aging:1996, Aging Into the 21st Century, p. 1)

Future Growth

The growth of the older population will slow during the 1990's, because of the small number of births during the depression years of the 1930's. The depression era babies are now reaching 65+, hence the decrease in the age cohort 65-74 years. The birth rate increased considerably from 1946-1964 (Baby boon cohorts). Based on Bureau of the Census population statistics released in 1996, we can project a moderate increase in the elderly population until about 2010 and a rapid increase from 2010-2030. See the following numerical projections for the 85 and over cohort:

    1995 - 3.6 million people
    2010 - 5.7 million people
    2030 - 8.5 million people
    2050 - 18.2 million people
(Administration on Aging:1996, Aging Into the 21st Century, p. 1-2)

Nursing Home Residents

Despite the previous demography, only five percent of the population of people over sixty-five years lived in nursing homes in 1990. However, the percentage of admissions increases with age. The dispersion ranges from one percent for persons sixty-five to seventy-four years to six percent for persons seventy-five to eighty-four years and twenty-four percent for eighty-five years and beyond. (Administration on Aging :1996, Aging Into the 21st Century, p. 4)

My next story pertains to a 70 year-old male patient, admitted to the hospital for surgery. He did not conform to institutional rules, and was described by hospital personnel as non-compliant and marginally confused. The nurses attributed his behavior to his age and unfamiliar surroundings.

The patient went to the operating room for a surgical procedure. After surgery he was returned to his hospital bed with a dressing on his lumbar region and several tubes to drain secretions. The patient was a retired tailor so he brought scissors, a possession related to his trade, to keep in his nightstand drawer. That evening he attempted to lie on his side, but he was hindered by his post-surgical tubing. To correct the problem, he used his scissors and cut the tubing. His actions created many problems.

I pose the following question: Did the labels confused and non-compliant bestowed on this patient hinder him from receiving an adequate explanation of what to expect after surgery? Did the assumption of impaired cognition impede the nurses and other health-team members from providing him with routine pre-operative teaching? What cues did they overlook, thereby, indirectly contributing to this drastic solution? Was it a problem of social organization? How was the scene arranged for the patient to display incompetence on such an important issue? According to Frake (1980), "The interpretation and treatment of illness is accomplished as a social behavior" (p. 119).

The aforementioned accounts characterize the events that prompted my interest in this study. My research, however, does not relate to the problems the elderly may face. Many earlier studies did (Carp, 1976; Cavan et al, 1949; Cumming & Henry, 1961; Neugarten, et al., 1964). Rather, my interest lies in the organization of talk. What we might call the cultural construction of aging. According to Frake (1980), if we want to find out what people know:

> We must get inside our subjects heads. This should not be an impossible feat: Our subjects themselves accomplished it when they learned their culture and became 'native actors.' They had no mysterious avenues of perception not available to us as investigators. (p. 27)

As stated earlier, it became apparent to me that the myths and labels used by members of the health team differed from those that were not part of it. I reflected on how significant this could be. According to Varenne (1986), "Culture is patterned action and as such is found in the practice of everyday life" (p. 34). If one is going to learn about people, one should go out into the many settings in which they conduct their lives. This is the pathway I choose to travel. I went to places to study people dealing with aging in various settings. The following is what I found.

NOTES

Frake, C.O. (1980). *Language and cultural description.* Stanford, CA: Stanford University Press.

McCabe, G.S., Fulk, C.H., & Staab, A.S. (1990). The Older person in the community. In A.Staab & M.Lyles (Eds.), *Manual of geriatric nursing.* Glenview Il: Scott, Foresman & Co.

Varenne, H. (1986). *Symbolizing America.* Lincoln: University of Nebraska Press.

II

Literature Review and Theoretical Framework

There is nothing to prepare you for the experience of growing old. Living is a process, an irreversible progression toward old age and eventual death. You see men of eighty still vital and straight as oaks; you see men of fifty reduced to gray shadows in the human landscape. The cellular clock differs for each one of us, and is profoundly affected by our own life experiences, our heredity, and perhaps most important, by the concepts of aging encountered in society and in oneself. (Curtin, 1972, p. 113)

Growing old is inevitable! The biological process of aging is the slow but continuous changes that occur between birth and death, that seem to be a feature of human life in all cultures.

Although everyone grows older, the particular ways individuals age and the meanings they attach to the life course are not universal. Also the way the life course is divided including the markers that delineate old age is highly variable. Our own cultural conceptions of age and aging are just that: our own. (Foner, 1984, p. 1)

Riley (1978) explained that the themes of aging may mold "personal plans, hopes and fears," (p. 2) as well as influence the way individuals in different cultures age. In fact they may effect the values associated with life and death.

This thesis reviews several areas of theory. The search included: (a) Literature on aging, which constitutes one area of information; (b) cultures, that is a people's way of living; (c) communication theory, which is what occurs when people interact or gather together in any situation; and (d) finally a glimpse at the social patterns of retirement. I decided to begin with a history of aging. As Chudacoff (1989) tells us, we live in an age conscious society and:

> Every person has an age; it is a direct, objective measure of the duration that someone has lived. Though we sometimes try to alter or distort age, it is an inescapable attribute of life; ultimately we cannot change or manipulate it as we change our weight, hair color or even sex. But in the past century or so, age has come to represent more than a chronological, biological phenomenon. It has acquired social meaning, affecting attitudes, behavior, and the ways in which individuals relate to each other. (p. 4)

Was America always an age conscious society? Did an awareness of age always dominate our society? According to Chudacoff this has not always been the case. Until the mid-19th century, Americans showed little concern with age! People were apt to forget their age, and birthdays were rarely celebrated. Children worked side by side with adults, and the one room schoolhouse was filled with children of varied ages. Chudacoff goes on to say that in the late 19th century age consciousness began to emerge in the United States. Schools began to set age limits, and pediatrics was established as a medical specialty. Concurrently with these changes, old age was identified as a separate stage of life, marked by specific age boundaries. Aging people were set apart from the rest of society, because it was assumed that they could not keep up with the demands of a scientifically progressive society.

Their opinion and experience was no longer necessary. Medical groups now equated deterioration of the mind (senile dementia) and physical deterioration of body organs as a normal occurrence of aging; especially in individuals who lived past seventy years. This concept led to the birth of old-age homes. Although only a small percentage of older people lived in these homes; it created barriers from the world they formerly enjoyed.

In the early years of the twentieth century, age norms increased, especially for young people. Age-peer organizations mushroomed; such as the gender specific scouts. After World War I, middle age was identified as a separate age norm in the American culture; and heightened consciousness of distinct stages of adulthood contributed to age-grading.

The 1930s hailed the advent of federal programs that used age as a criteria for the regulation of benefits. A prime example of this was the enactment of the Railroad Retirement Act in 1934, which in turn set the stage for the Social Security Act of 1935, with a designated age of 65 as an eligibility requirement for retirement benefits. In 1965, Congress created Medicare, which provided hospital insurance benefits for social security recipients; limited coverage of nursing home care; and low-cost voluntary insurance for all individuals sixty-five years and older to cover costs of physicians services, diagnostic tests, and some consultation services.

In addition, the Older Americans Act was initiated, which established an administration on aging to fund and coordinate programs for the aging, especially in the area of health and nutrition. This in turn led to the establishment of programs and legislation exclusively for the aging, and in turn juxtaposed with residential patterns that began to show increased isolation of older people from other age groups. More affluent aging people segregated themselves into retirement communities, where they purposely choose to live with age peers, especially in sun-belt regions such as Arizona and Florida. Individuals under fifty years were prohibited from renting or purchasing a home in these housing developments.

Concurrent with these patterns, life expectancies resulting from better medical care created new age grade systems in the social structure. Currently at least two age grade categories are recognized, the young aging, consisting of retired but energetic people generally up to 75 years; and the frail aging, those above 75. Media attention began to focus on incurable, chronic ailments such as Alzheimer's disease. This helped create negative stereotypes of aging people, especially in the frail aging category. Many studies were sponsored by the Institute on Aging. This served to inspire magazines and newspaper articles to focus on problems of aging. Magazines for an aging population began to emerge, such as *Harvest Years*; *Modern Maturity,* the magazine for the American Association of Retired Persons (AARP); and countless others. The entry of the term ageism in the common vocabulary signaled the advent of widespread stereotyping of people because of their chronological age (Chudacoff, 1989). In 1975, the age discrimination act was passed; this act outlaws discrimination based on age in all programs and institutions receiving federal funds, unless the program was originally designed for a specific age group.

Rossoe (1974) found aging people are commonly viewed in stereotypes. They are seen as representatives of an age group, not as individuals, and negative characteristics are attributed to them. It is interesting to note that these images of the aging are not limited to younger people alone, but are also shared by the aging themselves. Aging people de-value other aging persons. Furthermore, the stereotyped conceptions tend to be resistant to change, despite direct association.

Butler (1974) explains that, "to develop a clear depiction of what old age can be, we must contrast the mythologic with a realistic appraisal of old age" (p. 22). He shares the following stereotypes of aging:

An older person thinks and moves slowly. He does not think as he used to, nor as creatively. He is bound to himself and to his past and can no longer change or grow. He can neither learn well nor swiftly, and even if he could, he would not wish to. Tied to his personal traditions and growing conservatism, he dislikes innovations and is not disposed to new ideas. Not only can he not move forward, he often moves backwards. He enters a second childhood, caught often in increasing egocentricity and demanding more from his environment than he is willing to give to it. Sometimes he becomes more like himself, a caricature of a lifelong personality. He becomes irritable and cantankerous, yet shallow and enfeebled. He lives in his past. He is behind the times. He is aimless and wandering of mind, reminiscing and garrulous. Indeed, he is a study in decline. He is a picture of mental and physical failure. He has lost and cannot replace friends, spouse, jobs, status, power, influence, income. He is often stricken by diseases which in turn restrict his movement, his enjoyment of food, the pleasures of well being. His sexual interest and activity decline. His body shrinks; so, too, does the flow of blood to his brain. His mind does not utilize oxygen and sugar at the same rate as formerly. Feeble, uninteresting, he awaits his death, a burden to society, to his family, and to himself (p. 22).

Butler goes on to say that there are other major associated myths, including aging itself, and the idea of measuring one's age by the number of years one has lived. He believes the rates of metabolic and social aging are individual.

The second myth is unproductivity. Butler testifies that in the absence of diseases and social adversities, aging people tend to remain productive and involved in life. Butler also speaks of the third myth, which is disengagement. This will be discussed later under theories.

Fourth is the myth of inflexibility. Butler believes this has little to do with one's age, rather it has more to do with one's character, and barring brain destruction or illiteracy, people remain open to change throughout the course of their lifetime.

Fifth is the myth of senility. The notion that aging people become senile, evidenced by forgetfulness, episodes of confusion, and a reduced attention span, is widely accepted. Butler explains that senility is a layman's term, sometimes used by physicians to categorize the behavior of the old. Some of what is called senility is the result of brain damage. Also anxiety and depression are lumped in that category, even though they are treatable and reversible. It is beneficial to remember that aging people, like young people, experience a full range of emotional and disease states, including: anxiety, grief, malnutrition, unrecognized physical illnesses, late-life alcoholism, cerebral arteriosclerosis, and finally the overuse of drug tranquilization. Many of these conditions can cause a pseudo-senility.

Sixth is the myth of serenity. In contrast to the previous myth, this one portrays aging as an adult sainthood. Aging is described as a time of relative peace and serenity when people enjoy the fruits of their life-long labors, and peace and quiet prevails. Visions of white-haired grandmothers in rocking chairs are pictured by the younger generations. In reality, aging persons experience more stresses than any other age group. While the aging have a certain resiliency in some crisis situations, it should be noted that depressive reactions are quite common in late life, and "twenty-five percent of all suicides in the United States occur in persons over sixty-five" (Butler, 1974, p. 23). Butler urges society to take a more balanced view of aging. He contradicts the stereotypes by relating the following information: Aging people are as diverse as people of other periods in life, and their patterns of aging vary according to many variables. The majority of aging people live in the community and are ambulatory. Many physical and socio-economic forces interweave to contribute to the total picture of aging. Aging people tend to be reflective rather than impulsive. They have learned this lesson through life-experiences. Many are employable, productive and creative, and many enjoy leaving their mark through the young, as well as through ideas and institution (Butler, 1974).

Neugarten (1980) refuted the stereotypes and asserted her belief that "chronological age is becoming a poorer and poorer predictor of the way people live" (p. 157). The internal clock that dictated trends is not as powerful as it used to be, observed Neugarten, "no one says 'act your age' anymore" (p. 157).

On the positive side, Chudacoff (1989) believes that there are some advantages to living in an age-conscious society, such as providing the individual with a sense of belonging and a sense of self from an age based peer-group. This also enables policy makers to identify vulnerable groups, that is: infants, teenagers, middle-agers, the aging, and the frail aging who need selected types of government help.

The major disadvantage of such a society is the stereotype of ageism. Chudacoff (1989) goes on to say that "age cannot be changed" (p. 188), and to discriminate against individuals merely because they possess a particular characteristic offends the traditional American concept of fairness. As an example of this, Chudacoff points to a recent proposal by a biomedical ethicist, who suggests that life saving care be denied to aging people regardless of their state of health, if they are above a stated age.

Platt (1980) agreed with Chudacoff that industrialization stimulated many opportunities and afforded us many benefits. Yet, it also created new patterns of constraints as we move across the life span. However, he went on to say that it is time to take a renewed look at the biographical lines of human aging. "For the mature person is one of the most remarkable products that any society can bring forth (p.3)."

He cited East Asia as a strong believer in this concept, where the idea exists that people can go on improving with age. In addition, he explains that this idea existed as far back in history as Confucius. In the *Analects* the master says:

> At 15 I thought only of study; at 30 I began playing my role; at 40 I was sure of myself; at 50 I was conscious of my position in the universe; at 60 I was no longer argumentative; and now at 70 I can follow my heart's desire without violating custom. (Platt, 1980, p. 5)

Cowgill and Holmes (1972) identified eight universals of aging, although aging persons are always a minority group within the total population. This does not mean they are dominated by the majority; what it means is that aging is a key characteristic used by the members of a society to define themselves and others, even though the age groups could vary from one group to another. Aging in one society could be defined as everyone over 45, while in another society aging would be everyone over 70 years.

It is possible that the definition of aging in the United States could change in the next 50 to 100 years, as the numbers of people over 65 increase. Cross cultural studies indicate that age is not destiny, and that the social definition of aging fluctuates.

Because aging is an intimate part of life, it is recognized by all societies that the aging are in a position different from young people. While this may be a simple common-sense observation, it must be recognized that there are few universal properties in human societies. The fact that there is universal recognition of aging is important. In addition they are treated differently. Cowgill and Holmes explain that all societies have different cultural mores for dealing with aging individuals. For example, there are sets of expectations that govern the interaction of one aging individual with another, of one aging person with a younger person, and a young person with another young person.

There is a tendency for people defined as aging to move to more sedentary, supervisory, or governing types of roles that have less physical exertion, and are more concerned with group preservation and monetary production. This is manifested in industrial societies mainly by retirement from occupational endeavors; in non-industrial societies by allowing aging people to give up physically demanding activities. For example, the grandmother may give up household chores to the daughter-in-law, and take over the training of the children. The warrior may become a clergyman.

It should be noted that in all societies, some aging people continue to act as political leaders. I believe if one looks at our current world leaders we can identify this trend. This is evident in our own society in the form of Presidents, Chief Justices, Senators, and so on who are quite elderly. But these positions are not reserved for aging people. In non-industrial societies, some elevated positions are specifically delegated to aging people. According to Cowgill and Holmes (1972), one reason for this is that in non-industrial societies aging people have accumulated knowledge and information, are respected for this, and are valuable to society. In industrial societies rapid technology and social change make aging persons' knowledge obsolete, their information is not highly valued, therefore, they are not deemed anymore worthy of an exalted position than a younger person.

They suggested that in all societies the mores prescribe some mutual responsibility between old people and their adult children. However, there is a great difference in the social demands of the adult child/parent relationship. It is evident that there is some responsibility even in societies that emphasize the conjugal relationship over consanguinity and in societies in which the nuclear family takes precedence to the extended family. However, there are exceptions to the general rule; for instance, Turnbull (1977) reported that Ik, a tribe in Uganda gave up "all filial responsibilities during a severe drought that caused widespread starvation" (p. 73). "All societies value life and seek to prolong it, even in old age" (Cowgill & Holmes, 1972, p. 74). The fear of aging is most likely confined to young people, and most people are able to accommodate changes that occur with advancing age.

There is not a time when a general dissatisfaction with life occurs, and if people lose their desire to live, it is usually related to ill-health, the loss of friends or family members, or some other reason, not life itself.

In terms of variations in aging, Cowgill and Holmes (1972), have identified many, just by comparing industrial and pre-industrial societies. "Modernized societies have older populations, that have higher proportions of older people" (p. 74). Because the birth and death rates are higher in pre-industrial societies, the proportion of aging people is lower than industrial societies, that is if the aging population is defined in some chronological stage such as 60s and 70s.

It is believed that aging people have higher status in pre-industrial societies in which they constitute a lower proportion of the population and the rate of social change is slower. Recent studies have revealed that as society modernizes, the status of aging people decline. The individualistic value system of Western societies reduces the economic security of aging people and shifts the responsibility to the state to provide their economic security. In addition, the extended family concept and the family as a system of economic support is less available to aging people.

Laslett (1976), disputed the preceding concepts that there is a difference in the position of the aging in industrial societies as opposed to pre-industrial societies. He has discovered that the position of the aging in pre-industrial England, and probably in other places as well, was not what it is usually thought to have been. There is a possibility that gerontologists idealize the position of aging people in pre-industrial society. Laslett maintains that:

> There may be much more continuity in the preferred social position of older people than is usually imagined: 'The conclusion might be that then, as now, a place of your own, with help in the house, with access to your children, within reach of support, was what the elderly and the aged wanted for themselves in the pre-industrial world.' (1976, p. 76)

I will now discuss some of the major theories of aging.

THEORIES OF AGING

The activity theory is the oldest and probably the most widely accepted theory on aging. Essentially this theory states that the greater the activity of the individual, the greater the life satisfaction, and that this is true for all people of all ages. For the aging person this is even more important, because their health and social well-being are dependent on remaining active.

The theorists believe that people find the meaning of life through interaction. In essence, they stress the importance of people maintaining adequate levels of social activity if they are to age successfully. In addition, this will enable the individual to achieve a positive self-image and greater life satisfaction.

The activity theory was developed by a group of sociologists at the University of Chicago, and grew out of the concept of a roleless role of the aging (Burgess, 1960). In essence, Burgess viewed retired people as having "no vital function to perform" (p. 60); he believed this role was imposed on them at retirement, and they eventually accepted the role. "Although the activity theory was the first social theory of aging, it was only with the development of the disengagement theory that it became recognized as a distinct theory" (Decker, 1980, p. 137).

The premise of this theory is that aging people disengage from society. In describing disengagement, Cumming and Henry (1961) contend that it is normal for people to decrease their level of activity as they age; this is in direct contrast to the previous theory. Disengagement does not suggest a rocking chair for aging people; rather it suggests that they decrease their activity as they adapt to the normal changes of the aging process. Disengagement theory was presented in a functionalist framework, which was built upon previous research. The theorists saw people moving toward disengagement as they age, that is, they are gradually phased out of important roles in order for society to function; by doing this their death is not disruptive to the normal functioning of society.

The disengagement theorists acknowledged that although the process is inevitable, variations will occur because of biological differences. The theorists believed that high levels of satisfaction are associated with the aged's reduction of their roles. Since the inception of the theory, a lot of controversy has prevailed in the literature over its relevance and usefulness. In the last decade this theory as well as the activity theory have been supplemented by the age stratification and phenomenological theories of aging.

A third theory is the age stratification theory, (Riley, Johnson, & Foner 1972). This theory views society as composed of various age groups. Riley proposed a sociology of age stratification; she posited that age should not be viewed as an individual characteristic, but rather as a dynamic component of modern society. Riley's age stratum develops its own cohort as it moves through time and history. Therefore, patterns of aging can differ not only from one society to another, but also among successive cohorts in a society. According to Decker (1980), "Stratification Theory teaches us to analyze the functioning of a society in terms of cohorts or age groups that make up a society at any point in time" (p. 145).

Another social theory is the phenomenological and ethnographic case study approach of Jacobs, Gubrium, and Hochschild (1975) which is primarily concerned with the meaning of life and growing old. "The meaning these researchers are concerned with differ from the meaning social gerontologists attribute to aging, rather it is the meaning attributed to it by those who are doing the aging" (Decker, 1980, p. 146).

Whereas the disengagement theory uses a generalized process that is applicable to everyone, the phenomenological method individualizes the aging process; it sees persons as assigning their own meaning to aging, not that everyone has a unique view of aging. Many researchers recognized that we construct our meanings while interacting with others, and thus are influenced by them, but it does make people active participants in constructing and negotiating the meaning of aging.

The message for researchers is that we must be sensitive to the various settings and circumstances in which society assigns meaning to the aging process.

SUB-CULTURE THEORY

Rose proposed a different perspective on aging (Rose & Peterson, 1965). He noted that society's negative response to aging forced them to interact with each other despite a class division. According to Rose, the sub-culture creates a sense of group affiliation in the aging that prevails over all previous group memberships. A sub-culture may be an ethnic, economic, or a social group, which displays characteristics that distinguish its members from other groups within the culture. To support his idea of a sub-culture of the aging, he noted the increased number of people over 65, welfare programs directed toward this age group, the growth of retirement communities, and compulsory retirement. The sub-culture concept has been viewed more as a prediction of what might happen in the future than as a description of what has happened up until now.

Barron (1961) proposed the Minority Group Theory. He classifies the aging population as a minority group. Minority has been defined "as a group of people who because of physical or cultural characteristics are singled out from others in the society in which they live, for differential and unequal treatment, and who therefore regard themselves as objects of collective discrimination" (p. 61).

This would imply the existence of corresponding dominant groups with higher social status and more important privileges. Minority status carries with it the exclusion from full participation in the life of the society.

Barron (1961) believed that the aging person's overt physiological characteristics of aging render them susceptible to discrimination, similar to that which affects racial or sexual minority groups. Discrimination is facilitated, because the aging have no socially valid function, role, or activity pattern to fulfill.

Maddox (1973) refuted this theory "because of evidence which indicates that the aging are less disadvantaged than was once assumed" (p. 62). In addition, membership in the group known as aging is neither permanent nor exclusive. If anyone lives long enough he will join the group. According to Weinberger and Millham (1975), "The physical appearance of the aging is not enough to justify discriminatory treatment by others" (p. 62). For example, people who appear old are highly respected when they function as judges, physicians, legislators and in other prestigious positions. The idea that the aging are a minority group is not a useful framework for describing their status in society.

A study by Harris and Associates Inc., (1975), on *The Myths and Reality of Aging in America*, revealed the following findings: They refuted the concept of a homogenous aging population, in fact they underscored their differences. The findings indicated that there is no such thing as a typical aging person. People generally don't stop being themselves and suddenly turn into the old person, that fits society's myths and stereotypes. Instead, the psychosocial factors that effect people when they are young, persist throughout the life-cycle.

This section of the literature search addressed the social-historical path of aging, the major theories of aging, and a brief look at a study on the myths and reality of aging. Upon reflecting on this brief history of social gerontology and theories, it is evident that some efforts have been made to deal with the dilemma of studying the aging process, and it is comforting to note that some areas of research have addressed the myths and stereotypes of aging. This part of the literature is relevant to this research, as well as segments of the phenomenological and ethnographic theory by Jacobs, Gubrium and Hochschild (1975). It is now time to progress to the cultural section of the literature search.

THE SIGNIFICANCE OF CULTURE

Culture provides principles for framing experience as eventful in particular ways, but it does not provide one with a set of event-types to map into the world. Culture is not simply a cognitive map that people acquire, in whole or in part, more or less accurately, and then learn to read. People are cast out into imperfectly charted, continually shifting seas of everyday life. Mapping them out is a constant process resulting not in an individual cognitive map, but in a whole chart case of rough, improvised continually revised sketch maps. Culture does not provide a cognitive map, but rather a set of principles for mapping and navigation. Different cultures are like different schools of navigation designed to cope with different terrains and seas. (Frake, 1980, p. 58)

This section of the literature was enlightened by the previous text; it reinforced the notion that there are boundaries and constraints when doing research. One is dealing with a culturally defined population, not a neat set of principles that will provide prescriptive solutions. Most of the research on aging that I analyzed was dealt with in a reflexive fashion, and limited to variables the researchers deemed important (Carp, 1976, Cumming & Henry 1961, Neugarten, 1964) to name a few. Essentially, our culture provides us with a way of viewing the world; it characterizes the cradle of humanity that people live in, we are enchanted by it. Anthropologists call this culture-bound.

Amoss (1981) attempted to distinguish culture and society as separate and distinct systems, each operating by its own rules. She followed Parsons and Geertz's definition, by defining (culture) as a gloss for "an ordered system of meaning and of symbols in terms of which social interaction takes place and society as the pattern of social interaction itself" (p. 48). Amoss identified two universal themes attached to aging. One being the association between aging and death. This theme has unfortunately created a perception of aging as fearful and threatening. The second theme has a more positive implication, in comparison with the young, the old represent culture as opposed to nature. Amoss credited Levi-Strauss with finding this nature/culture distinction to be a widespread element in myth, and has pointed out how many myths celebrate the transformation of humankind from a state of nature to a state of culture, by focusing on the gift of the hearth fire and the origins of cooked food (p. 49). Amoss (1981) believed this information can be used positively for favorable cultural evaluation of the aging, because they are the people that carry the cultural traditions and are the masters of "rhetoric and oral literature" (p. 49).

According to Geertz (1968), "Non-cultured humans do not exist, never have existed, and more important could not in the nature of the case exist" (p. 52). Essentially Geertz posited that individuals or society as a whole could not survive without culture. Previously it was acknowledged that we are constrained by the culture, but does it mean that we are captives of our culture?

Karl Marx (1969) addressed this issue in the following context: "Men make their own history, but they do not make it just as they please; they make it under circumstances directly encountered, given, and transmitted from the past" (p. 73).

As individuals, we cannot change cultural patterns; collectively we do it all the time.

According to the anthropological accounts of Amoss and Harrell (1981), old age is recognized as a distinct life stage in a wide variety of cultures. Some anthropologists believe this is universal. Cowgill (1972) stated that "some people are considered 'old' in all societies, and they are associated with specific roles" (p. 4). Amoss and Harrell (1981) write, "Every known society has a named social category of people who are old. In every case these people have different rights, duties, privileges and burdens from those enjoyed or suffered by their juniors." (p. 3)

"What is not constant, of course, are the criteria by which people decide who is old, or the sharpness of the boundaries marking off old age" (Foner, 1984, p. 8).

Claude Levi-Strauss (1981) (cited in P. Amoss & S. Harrell, 1981) talked about aging and culture in the following text:

> The young are to the old as culture is to nature. Levi-Strauss proposed that a dichotomy between the humanly created world culture and the natural environment is present in the conceptual map of every human culture represented in myths and religious ritual. (p. 15)

The themes of myths and ritual are found in several of the works of Levi-Strauss. In view of their relevance to the aging population, they represent a useful aspect of the literature review. Benedict (1934) identified *patterns of culture* and the theory of an individual's culture as an aggregate of the whole.

According to Cantor (1980), another important theme about people in most cultures includes the balancing of dependent and independent needs. Many traditional values center on the ability of the individual to survive successfully, with a minimum of assistance from others. This ethos still pervades our culture and remains a standard against which society measures the individual's worth.

From the life cycle perspective there are two stages when the culture accepts dependency needs, at the beginning of the cycle and at the end of the cycle. It is considered appropriate for infants and children to be nurtured by parents, and again as persons grow older. However, in the case of aging, as the balance shifts from independence to dependence, the potential for conflict arises. This presents a dilemma for the individual, deeply rooted cultural norms of independence and self-sufficiency on one hand, and the need for assistance on the other, as health and other physical attributes decline.

This raises the question, how can such conflicting values be resolved with dignity for the individual? Who is most appropriately seen as the preferred avenue of assistance? Do different needs and different stages of aging require different modalities of care? Cantor (1980) believed this is where a knowledge of kinship structure and the relation of the informal support systems to formal organizations is essential, if people working with older people are to play a positive role in helping them resolve their dependency crises. In retrospect, the research indicates that aging people turn first to their children, then friends and neighbors, and only after these systems are exhausted or are not available do they turn to formal organizations. It is these significant others who comprise the basis for the social support systems for the aging population in the United States.

Trends toward smaller families, increased life-span, working women, and fluctuating mobility of all ages, suggest important implications for children being a primary resource for aging family members.

In a study by Kivett and Atkinson (1984), it was discovered that the number of children in a family is related to the number of visits aging parents receive, and also the amount of help they can expect. This also included financial help. Parents with an only child can expect fewer visits, especially if the child is employed. The study also revealed that aging parents expect children to assume some responsibility for health, economic, and emotional needs, regardless of how many offspring there are to share the assistance. These demands make it difficult for middle-aged children with many family, career stresses, and responsibilities, to meet the expectations of the aging parents. Daughters provided more assistance and have more association with parents than sons. Parents receive more monetary assistance as the income of their offspring increases.

Ethnicity is also a factor. For instance, in Asian families, the aging members are held in esteem and the young people defer to them. Likewise, they provide a home for their aging parents in retirement. With African Americans, aging and death are viewed as a normal process of everyday living. In this culture, the aging members are also held in esteem.

In a similar type of study, Thomas (1988) found that parents may tend to expect less help from children that live at a distance. In addition, they appreciate most the help that keeps them autonomous and functioning independently. The study also revealed that parents with increased ill-health express less satisfaction with their children's help, possibly because it places them in a dependent position.

Childless couples, and those single aging individuals without family support are especially vulnerable at crisis points, such as episodes of illness, or loss of a significant other.

Continuing with the community, Fennel (1981) reported that "traditional anthropological 'holism' in the community studies has only begun to offer its valuable perspective to gerontological inquiries" (p. 132). Until this is done sufficiently, adequate understanding of the majority of the aging population, especially those living in the community, will be deficient. She informs us that aging people generally live within the larger communities in cooperation, and also in conflict, with those of other age groups, "all being differently esteemed, assigned tasks, and allowed privileges, partly on the basis of age" (p.132). Fennel advised society that it is impossible to understand the social conditions of the aging, without viewing them within this broader age-integrated context.

In relation to the culture of the institutionalized aging, Faulwell and Pomeranz (1981) launched a study on physician influence in the selection of institutionalization of aging clients. In essence, the results of their study indicate that medical students in general are mainly exposed to treatment of acute rather than chronic illnesses, and as such, are ill-prepared to meet the chronic health needs of the aging. Furthermore, medical students are rarely exposed to aging individuals who are active and independent in the community, therefore, their education does not prepare them to deal with the realities of the majority of the aging population. The study suggests that medical education recognize the significance of restorative care for the aging population, and begin to emphasize a more positive biopsychosocial approach. This, in turn, may prevent the physician from delegating their care to an institution when confronted with a patient he cannot cure.

In general, the results of the study revealed three factors which appear to influence the physician's decision: (a) cultural fit of the physician and client, (b) the physician's length of association with the client, and (c) the method of patient referral to the physician.

Addressing the care of the institutionalized aging, Schmit and Jones (1981), described a comparison study. They compared two long-term care facilities (commonly referred to as nursing homes). One institution was located in the United States and the other in Scotland. The findings indicated that in the American facility "the elderly are infantilized, depersonalized, dehumanized, and victimized by their caretakers," (p. 250) while at the Scottish institution "these phenomena were not seen" (p. 250). The researchers believed it was important to discover why this takes place at one environment and not the other; they hypothesized that the exchange theory might offer an explanation. Dowd (1975), (cited in Schmit and Jones, 1981) has posited a view of aging as a system of social exchange. He sees the problem of aging as one of decreasing control over power resources. "As power resources decline, the aged unable to engage in balanced exchange relations are forced to exchange compliance for their continued sustenance" (p. 250).

In relation to aging in the American institution, this theory was relevant. Due to chronic physical disability, mental impairment, and in some cases, lack of relatives and friends, many are dependent on the staff for multiple services. They have few resources with which to reciprocate, therefore, they are forced to comply with the rules of the staff.

The clients in the Scottish institution had more resources to exchange (i.e., items made in diversional therapy). In addition, the findings indicated that the American institution suffered from a lack of professional leadership (doctors and nurses) for the care of the aging. Furthermore, the proprietor needs to make a profit, and the "financing and delivery of health care in our society forces the elderly into dependency" (p. 253). The researchers believe the "Scottish model of Geriatric Care provides an excellent example of quality long-term care" (p. 254).

According to the literature, we are an aging society. Scientific discovery and technical progress have lengthened our life expectancy. However, this increased life expectancy extracts a price. We as a society are challenged to insure a dignified quality of life for all. Are we aging with dignity, or are we afraid of depleting our economic resources and being a burden on our children or society. Are we afraid of going to a hospital and subsequently a nursing home? Have we allowed the stereotypes to cloud the truth? Have we constructed a cultural border? Aging is something we share; it does not seem to be a dichotomous world—the aging and the non-aging.

This completes my cultural review of the literature. While my search was not exhaustive, I felt it gave me adequate insight into the culture of aging. Stated another way, Varenne (1977) writes, "To write a grammar a linguist needs only a set of sentences and a few informants, I think this is all one needs to describe a culture" (p.229).

I will now proceed to Communication Theory.

COMMUNICATION

When we talk about communication we discuss it as a complex and sustaining system through which various members of the society interrelate with more or less efficiency and facility. (Birdwhistell, 1970a, p. 12)

Communication does not simply happen in a mysterious, extrasensory fashion. It is a set of definite, concrete behaviors which people perform and which they can be observed to perform. (Varenne, 1983, p. 70)

It is evident that communication is a complex process and plays a major role in the individual's everyday life. It includes three levels of interaction and is society's social matrix. "Meaning is communicated each time one member of a society interacts with another member; this is described as a cultural event. When members of different cultures interact, dissimilar verbal, kinesis, and proxemic cues can contribute to misunderstandings" (Pasquali, Arnold, DeBasio, p. 279).

Birdwhistell (1963, 1970), "recognized certain similarities between spoken, written, and body language. His research was guided by two basic assumptions: that individuals are constantly maneuvering to accommodate the presence and activities of other individuals, and that

the system of kinesic movement is learned and ultimately analyzable."
He also believed kinesic behavior is culturally variable (p. 283).

The proxemic level of communication, the use of space, is
explained by Scheflen and Ashcraft (1976) as bounded space claimed
by a person through body language. As language evolves and attempts
are made to clarify speech, body motions such as gestures, posturing,
and spacing behavior begin to be used.

Considering the aforementioned communication theory, I am
aware of Elkman and Friesen's (1971) words that "the facial
expressions that convey such basic emotions as anger, fear, sadness,
amusement, puzzlement and disgust, are culturally universal; they are
innate in our species, and socialized in any culture" (p. 123).

While Elkman and Friesen addressed the afore-mentioned overt
expressions, Birdwhistell (1970b) described the following covert
communication:

> The human face is capable of 250,000 different expressions, many of
> them extremely subtle. The head, fingers, hands, arms, shoulders,
> trunk, hips, and legs, can all be used to signify meaning. All these
> potential sources of communication can be used in multiple
> combinations, meaning that literally millions of messages can be
> transmitted through the language of body movement. If two people
> were enclosed in a box and every aspect of their behavior recorded
> down to microscopic levels, it would be possible to isolate as many
> as 5000 separate bits of information every second. (p. 123)

In studying people, non-verbal communication plays a very
important role. For example, the male population of this vintage rarely
cry. Yet one wonders how they express grief and sadness. In my
practice I have noticed that some tend to drop their jaw, others tend to
shift it sideways, perhaps it relates to the old theory of maintaining a
stiff upper lip. Or what about the individuals that sit with their arms
folded and their legs crossed, are they being closed, or is it a relaxing
comfortable position for them? To answer this question one would
have to assess the situation further. We can learn a lot from body
language as described in the above passages, this information was
helpful to me when interviewing informants.

The afore-mentioned text was classified as symbols. Perhaps the most useful and adaptable of all symbols are written and spoken words. Every language has socially agreed upon words, as Varenne (1983) stated, "Just as time and uncertainty are at the core of human experience, so is talk, talk that is not divorced from action, but on the contrary, that is intimately tied with it" (p. 18).

The discussion of communication brings to mind Bakhtin's (1986) suggestions:

All words are tainted with conceptual overtones;
the individuals words are not his own; all words are
half someone else's.
        The angle of vision is always through someone else.
Language lies only in the dialogic interaction of those who
make use of it; people speak in many voices.

In reference to conversation, Bakhtin states:

Every conversation is full of transmissions
and interpretations of other peoples words
at every step one meets a quotation or a
reference to something that a particular
person said, a reference to "people say" or
"everyone says" to the words of the person
one is talking with, or to one's previous
words, to a newspaper, a book, and so forth.
The majority of our information and opinions
are usually communicated in direct form, as
our own, but with reference to some indefinite
and general source. (p. 338)

Both references were helpful to my research. Through language the actor may produce verbal negotiations that implement cultural actions. Pertaining to Bakhtin this reference encouraged me to continually assess my own cultural biases and references when communicating with informants. Byers (1985a) sees communication as:

> More than exchanging messages or getting one's point across. It is the process by which all the pieces of the living world find their relationships to the other pieces to form larger wholes and to enable the living world to grow, adapt, and survive (p. 71).

In this article Byers writes about sharing communication in groups, which he describes as cooperation when two or more people come together to interact. This emerges into a relationship that is a third higher level entity. To explain this concept, Byers uses marriage as an example, that is, a married person relates not only to a spouse, but to a higher order—the marriage. Byers believes many societal problems are traceable to a misunderstanding in cooperation. When I first met with informants we were at the level of negotiation. As the interviews progressed I believe we were at the level of cooperation. Byers (1985a) goes on to say that one person can produce language by himself. However a conversation requires at least two people, and in that context, "One person is not doing (saying) things to the other. They are organizing each other by means of language and other things" (p. 29).

In a different framework, Goffman (1974) discussed communication in the context of frames. He believed that "when the individual speaks, he avails himself of certain options and forgoes others, operating within a frame space" (p. 10). For the person to speak acceptably he must remain within that frame. Frake (1980) described frames as a useful methodological tool for obtaining and organizing certain kinds of data. Framing questions will be discussed in the methodology chapter. All aspects of the theory have contributed in some way to the research described in subsequent chapters.

I will now proceed to retirement.

SOCIAL PATTERNS OF RETIREMENT

In concluding this discussion of the literature relevant to aging in society, it seems appropriate to mention retirement. In a society with increasing life expectancy, retirement becomes an issue for most individuals. Since the advent of the Railroad Retirement Act and the

Social Security Act in the 1930s, 65 has been an accepted standard for retirement. In 1983, Congress took steps to gradually increase the age for these benefits. In addition, the mandatory retirement age was eliminated for most workers. Despite these measures which allows most Americans to work to a more advanced age, the trend toward early retirement is increasing. 60 to 62 is a typical retirement age today. The exception is blue collar workers, who seek relief from physically draining work; mid-to-late 50s is not an uncommon retirement age for some.

Another noticeable trend is the involvement of older people in second careers and the pursuit of higher education. Retirement is no longer associated with disengagement from life. Women as well as men are active participants in these changing trends and visa versa. The notion of retiring or continuing to work is not a matter of choice for all workers. Many people are forced to retire before they had anticipated such action. This is supposedly related to economic constraints in business and industry. The pie is usually sweetened for the retiree by adding a number of years to their pension vesture, until they reach the accepted age of 65 years. The pattern that induced the individual to retire will strongly influence his or her adjustment. All patterns involve role changes, which usually require adjustment.

Thomas Jefferson wrote in 1794 "that he eagerly awaited the time of life when he would exchange the roars and tumults of the bulls and bears for the prattles of my grandchildren and senile rest" (senile in quote, neutral adjective referring to the quality of being old) (Chudacoff, 1989, p. 57). Does this theme still prevail for today's retirees? Drawing from the literature, most people are satisfied with their lives in retirement. However, people who remain active have greater levels of satisfaction in their lives.

Finally, it seems appropriate to turn to an author, Barbara Myerhoff, (1978) who gives voice to the aging in her portrayal of *Number Our Days*. This is a touching, and uplifting account of elderly Jewish people in an urban neighborhood. A major strength of the study was the description of Jewish culture and language and how these shared similarities provided strength and encouragement in their lives. Additionally, Myerhoff noted that dignity and autonomy were important issues for this population of elderly people. This concept was expressed in the form of supporting others more needy than they, despite the fact that most of them lived on a meager income. Perhaps her message is most succinctly communicated by her story of Jacob, a 95 year old man, who delivers his final message to his friends in a birthday speech:

> Dear friends: Every other year I have had something significant to say, some meaningful message when we come together for this yontif. But this year, I don't have an important message. I don't have the strength. . . . It is very hard for me to accept the idea that I am played out. . . . . Nature has a good way of expressing herself when bringing humanity to the end of its years, but when it touches you personally it is hard to comprehend. I do have a wish for today. . . . It is this: that my last five years, until I am one hundred, my birthday will be celebrated here with you. . . . Whether I am here or not. It will be an opportunity for the members of my beloved Center to be together for a simcha and at the same time raise money for our beleaguered Israel. . . . (p. 164)

Myerhoff, goes on to say that the message was powerful in its verbal and nonverbal content. The gentleman's passion to be heard and to complete his purpose was his strongest communication. He was demonstrating what he had said in previous interviews, "that he sustained himself as an autonomous, lucid person, using thinking, speaking, and writing as his shields against dissolution and despair" (1978, p. 164).

NOTES

Amoss, P. T. (1981). Cultural centrality and prestige for the elderly: The coast salish case. In C.L. Fry (Eds.), *Dimensions: aging, culture, and health.* (pp. 47-63). New York: J.F. Bergin Publishers, Inc.

Amoss, P., & Harrell, S. (1981). An anthropological perspective on aging. In P. Amoss & S. Harrell, (Eds.), *Other ways of growing old.* (pp. 3-4). Stanford, CA: Stanford University Press.

Bakhtin, M.M. (1986). *The dialogic imagination.* Austin: University of Texas Press.

Barron, M.L. (1961). Minority group theory. In A.G. Yurick, S.S. Robb, B.E. Spier, & N.J. Ebert (Eds.), *The aged person and the nursing process.* (pp.61-62). New York: Appleton-Century-Crofts.

Birdwhistell, R. L. (1963). Properties of kinesic behavior. In P.N. Debasio (Ed.), *Mental health nursing.* (pp.283-289). St. Louis, Baltimore and Toronto: C.V. Mosby Company.

Birdwhistell, R.L. (1970a). *Kinesics and context.* Philadelphia: University of Pennsylvania Press.

Birdwhistell, R. L. (1970b). Body language. In I. Robertson. (Ed.), *Sociology.* New York: Worth Publishers, Inc.

Burgess, E.W. (1960). Retirement as a social role. In R.C. Atchley. (Ed.), *The Sociology of Retirement.* (pp.60-73). New York: John Wiley & Sons.

Butler, R.N. (1974). Successful aging and the role of life review. In S.H. Zarit. (Ed.), *Readings in aging and death: Contemporary perspectives.* (2nd ed.), (pp.22-26). New York: Harper & Row, Publishers. Reprinted by permission of Addison-Wesley Educational Publications Inc.

Byers, P. (1985a). Communication: Cooperation or negotiation? *Theory into practice.* (pp.1,24,29,71).

Cantor, M.H. (1980). The informal support system: Its relevance in the lives of the elderly. In E.F. Borgatta & N.G. McCluskey (Eds.), *Aging and society.* (pp.131-144). Beverly Hills, CA: Sage Publications Inc.

Carp, F.H. (1976). Housing and living environments of older people. In R.H. Binstock & E. Shanas (Eds.), *Handbook of aging and the social sciences.* (pp.244-271). New York: Van Nostrand Reinhold Company.

Chudacoff, H.P. (1989). *How old are you?: Age consciousness in American culture.* (pp.10,44-45,57-59,65,104,107,111,115,180-181*).* Princeton, NJ: Princeton University Press.

Cowgill, D.O. (1972). What is old age? In N. Foner (Ed.), *Ages in conflict.* (pp.1-27). New York: Columbia University Press.

Cowgill, D.O., & Holmes, L.D. (1972). The universals of aging. In D.L. Decker (Ed.), *Social gerontology.* (pp.70-93). Boston: Little Brown and Company.

Cumming, E., & Henry, W.E. (1961). *Growing old: The process of disengagement.* New York: Basic Books.

Curtin, S. (1972). Aging in the land of the young. In S.H. Zarit (Ed.), *Readings in aging and death: Contemporary perspectives* (2nd ed.). (p.113). New

York: Harper & Row, Publishers. Reprinted by permission of Addison-Wesley Educational Publications Inc.

Decker, D.L. (1980). *Social gerontology.* Boston: Little Brown and Company.

Elkman, P., & Friesen, W.B. (1971). Body language. In I. Robertson (Ed.), *Sociology.* (pp. 122-123). New York: Worth Publishers Inc.

Faulwell, M., & Pomerantz, R.S. (1981). Physician influence in the selection of institutionalization of the elderly. In C.L. Fry (Eds.), *Dimensions: Aging, culture and health.* (pp. 219-232). New York: J.F. Bergin Publishers, Inc.

Fennel, V. (1981). Friendship and kinship in older women's organizations: Introduction. In C.L. Fry (Eds.), *Dimensions: Aging, culture, and health.* (pp. 131-143). New York: J.F. Bergin Publishers Inc.

Foner, N. (1984). *Ages in conflict: A cross cultural perspective on inequality between old and young.* New York: Columbia University Press.

Frake, C.O. (1980a). *Language and cultural description.* Stanford, CA: Stanford University Press.

Geertz, C. (1968). The impact of the concept of culture on the concept of man. In I. Robertson (Ed.), *Sociology.* (pp.51-60). New York: Worth Publications, Inc.

Goffman, E. (1974). *Frame analysis.* Cambridge, Ma: Harvard University Press.

Harris, L. & Associates, Inc. (1975). *The myth and reality of aging in America.* Washington, DC: The National Council on Aging.

Jacobs, J., Gubrium, J., & Hochschild, A.R. (1975). The phenomenological theory. In D.L. Decker (Ed.), *Social gerontology.* Boston: Little Brown and Co.

Kivett, V., & Atkinson M. (1984). Relationships with offspring and other family members. In R.B. Murray & J.P. Zentner (Eds.), *Nursing assessment & health promotion strategies through the life span.* Englewood Cliffs, NJ: Appleton and Lange.

Laslett, P. (1976). Variations in aging. In D.L. Decker (Ed.), *Social gerontology.* Boston: Little Brown and Company.

Levi-Strauss, C. (1981). An anthropological perspective on aging. In P. Amoss & S. Harrell (Eds.), *Other ways of growing old.* Stanford: Stanford University Press.

Maddox, G.L. (1973). Minority group theory. In A.G. Yurick, S.S. Robb, B.E. Spier, & N.J. Ebert (Eds.), *The Aged person and the nursing process.* New York: Appleton-Century-Crofts.

Marx, K. (1969). Are we prisoners of culture? In I. Robertson (Ed.), *Sociology.* New York: Worth Publishers, Inc.

Meyerhoff, B. (1978). Teach us to number our days. In S.H. Zarit (Ed.), *Readings in aging and death: Contemporary perspectives.* (2nd ed.) New York: Harper & Row Publishers.

Neugarten, B. (1980). "Acting one's age": New rules for old. In H.P. Chudacoff (Ed.), *How old are you?: Age consciousness in American culture.* Princeton, NJ: Princeton University Press.

Pasquali, E.A., Arnold, M.H., & Debasio, N. (1989). *Basic concepts of communication in mental health nursing: a holistic approach.* St.Louis: The C.V. Mosby Company.

Platt, D.W. (1980). *Long engagements.* Stanford, CA: Stanford University Press.

Riley, M.W. (1978). Definitions of old age: Some problems. In N. Foner (Ed.), *Ages in conflict.* New York: Columbia University Press.

Riley, M.W., Johnson, M., & Foner, A. (1972). *Aging and society.* Vol. 3, A Sociology of Age Stratification. New York: Russell Sage.

Rose, A., & Peterson, W. (1965). *Older people and their social world—The subculture of aging.* Philadelphia: F.A. Davis.

Rossoe, I. (1974). *Socialization to old age.* Berkeley, CA: University of California Press.

Scheflen, A.E., & Ashcraft, N. (1976). *Human territories: How we behave in space-time.* Englewood Cliffs, NJ: Prentice-Hall, Inc.

Schmit, J., & Jones, K. (1981). Quality of care for the institutionalized aged: A Scottish-American comparison. In C. L. Fry (Eds.), *Dimensions: Aging, culture and health.* New York: J.F. Bergin Publishers, Inc.

Thomas, J. (1988). Predictors of satisfaction with children's help for younger and older elderly parents. *Journal of Gerontology: Social Sciences.* 43 (1)., 9-14.

Turnbull, C.M. (1977). The universal's of aging. In D.L. Decker (Ed.), *Social gerontology.* Boston: Little Brown and Co.

Varenne, H. (1977). *Americans together: Structured diversity in a midwestern town.* New York: Teachers College Press.

Varenne, H. (1983). *American school language: Culturally patterned conflicts in a suburban high school.* New York: Irvington Publishers, Inc.

Weinberger, L.E., Millham, J. (1975). Minority group theory. In A. G. Yurick, S.S. Robb, B.E. Spier, & N.J. Ebert (Eds.), *The aged person and the nursing process*. New York: Appleton-Century-Crofts.

III

Methodology

This is an ethnography conducted in several selected settings in the community. The premise of the study is that aging is a label, and a set of myths, and that this myth is part of the conditions of growing old in American Society. The settings will be described later.

To many people, aging is something that happens to a person when they reach 65 years and start to collect Social Security, but to the individual it is a much more complex process. It is a world of cultural meaning that he or she must deal with in order to carry out her daily living in society. In this study I want to explore the language that governs the myth of aging, the properties of this myth, the occasions when the myth creates tension, and their mode of expression.

Culture refers to beliefs, values and practices of a particular group of people, that are learned, shared and passed on from one generation to the next. These cultural patterns guide thinking and decision making. Stated another way, culture is viewed by Varenne (1977) as "a certain level of human action that possesses its own structuring processes" (p. 218). I chose the ethnographic method because it permitted me to interact with the informants on a person to person level in their own surrounds. The approach has been persuasively addressed by Varenne (1983) in the following passage: "A central goal of ethnography is a multifaceted account of events happening in a particular location. Rigor in ethnography, if not validity, lies in the attempt to capture an event from many different points of view" (p. 9).

In addition, it provides an open-ended narrative method of collecting data without trying to fit informants experiences into pre-determined concepts. I did not expect an ethnography to answer a lot of compelling questions about the aging population, but I believed it provided a completely different way of exploring references to aging. The analysis was conducted from a structuralist framework. According to Gardner (1974), "Structuralism is a method of approach rather than a carefully formulated catechism. Structuralism is an attempt to discern the arrangements of elements underlying a given domain" (p. 12).

Levi-Strauss tells us that "the universals of human culture exist only at the level of structure, never at the level of manifest fact" (p. 22).

Byers (1985b) believes structuralists are less interested in things than in the organization which serves to create them and in the way things are organized to create larger, more complex things.

METHOD

The method I used for this study incorporated many of the interviewing techniques I use in my professional role as a nurse. I wanted to seek out ordinary individuals; and establish rapport with them, through a warm and friendly approach. I wanted the interviews to occur in the informants surroundings. Additionally, the informants were advised of the purpose of the interview, prior to its implementation. As well as inscription of the interview; by written mode, or if appropriate to tape record the interview. I wanted the interviews to focus on the research topic in a relaxed fashion. I constructed my questions to complement this approach, in terminology familiar to the informants. While I was astute to the individuals common cultural patterns; I did not categorize them according to their cultural background. According to Wilson (1993), "Qualitative research methods and qualitative analysis aspire to capture what other people and their lives are about without preconceiving the categories into which information will fit" (p. 216).

The data gathering took place over a one and a half-year period. My initial effort in data gathering included conducting several pilot interviews with individuals prior to gathering my actual data. I believe this enabled me to function more effectively as an interviewer. I also elicited help from my friends by obtaining two taped interviews from two distant geographical locations, one interview took place in Mississippi, and one in Ireland. While the information was helpful in providing insight into the culture of aging in other places, it was not adequately connected to this research. I also attended a high school forensic group that presented a debate on the needs of the aging population. I wanted to know how their discussion on this subject was organized. Since my interest lay in finding those moments where age-grading exists and the dialogue it represents, I realized the information was not relevant to my research. Had I been interested in studying the dynamics of aging or the psychosocial aspects of aging, I would have made a different choice.

I then turned to the media. I was interested in the way aging is depicted in both television text and other popular written sources. This helped me in identifying the common themes of aging. Chapter IV will discuss this data. Since I was interested in how cultural categories were made relevant to aging, I went to various locations and used participant observation, as I realized that social construction is done in many places. I decided to place myself in a situation where it is done naturally. This content will also be described in Chapter IV.

The preceding sources of information, as well as many informal interviews, helped me identify the settings for my actual research. My actual data collection included the following: (a) An interview with a 92 year-old woman who currently maintains her own residence, (b) an interview with an 83 year-old woman in her apartment, (c) an interview with a young mother whose father was recently placed in a nursing home, (d) an interview with a resident from an Adult Community Residence (this adult community was selected out of three residences), and finally (e) a taped discussion of aging by a group of friends in a home who were gathered together for a holiday dinner. In these settings I believed I would find the true patterns of aging.

The five settings were selected by me after careful consideration. I attempted to select settings that produced age-talk with a diversified flavor. They will be described in detail in subsequent chapters.

At this time I believe it is appropriate to say that the names and places of the informants were changed to protect their anonymity. They were also informed that their right to privacy would be protected in every possible way, even if this meant sacrificing the data.

Before turning to the language of aging in the media and the particular settings, I want to take a moment to discuss the strengths and limitations of this study.

While most of the people discussed in this study were 65 years of age and above, the informants were not limited to this age group. Clearly this is a strength of the study, as it provided a more diversified group of informants to contribute data. The informants I interviewed were limited to white, middle-class adults; however, several people were from multi-ethnic backgrounds.

In implementing any fieldwork, there are certain boundaries and constraints. As Varenne (1972) writes, "The bounding of a population is dependent on a decision grounded outside the methodology" (p. 225). The population of informants were selected from the community and long term care facilities. Other areas were omitted, including individuals hospitalized in acute care settings, nutrition and recreation centers for senior citizens, participants in continuing education classes, and the list goes on. While children were part of the community of some of the ethnographic settings and were non-verbal participants, I did not directly use them as informants.

The data chosen for my analysis was solely based on my preference, providing it met certain appropriate criteria, germane to my thesis. Consequently, there may be limitations to the depth of the work, despite a conscientious attempt to present a comprehensive analysis. In addition, the analysis of an informants data will not completely reveal the cognitive world of its members, but perhaps an important slice of it. As Varenne (1977) tells us, "A culture is not something to be easily transcended" (p.232).

Would I be able to think like my informants? Is it possible for a beginning ethnographer to surmount these obstacles? One hopes so. However, considering the human element, it would seem that a certain hint of bias and reflexivity would persist in most encounters. According to Schultz (1959), "The person assumes, that the other person assumes as well, and assumes that as he assumes it of the other person, the other person assumes the same for him" (p. 55).

Another variable is the concept of time. As stated in a previous chapter, the study took place over a one-and-a-half year period. Varenne (1977) cautions that a study has a time value, in that its validity is actually limited to the moment in which it was done.

Despite the aforementioned limitations, my firm conviction is that my findings are just that, my findings. This concurs with a statement in a previous chapter about cultural conceptions. However, regardless of some tainted hindrances, *I believe* the study will in some important way amplify the voices of the elderly by untangling the cultural myths that frame them.

NOTES

Byers, P. (1985b) Conversation: A context for language. *Gaikokugo Kyoiku.* (pp.*13*, 27-30).

Gardner, H. (1974). *The quest for mind: Piaget, Levi-Strauss and the structuralist movement.* New York: Vintage Books.

Levi-Strauss, C. (1981). An anthropological perspective on aging. In P. Amoss & S. Harrell (Eds.), *Other ways of growing old.* Stanford: Stanford University Press.

Schultz, A. (1959). Common sense and scientific interpretations of human action. In H. Garfinkel (Ed.), *Studies in ethnomethodology.* New York: Prentice-Hall, Inc.

Varenne, H. (1977). *Americans together: Structured diversity in a midwestern town.* New York: Teachers College Press.

Varenne, H. (1983). *American school language: Culturally patterned conflicts in a suburban high school.* New York: Irvington Publishers, Inc.

Wilson, H.S. (1993). *Introducing research in Nursing.* 2nd ed. California: Addison-Wesley Nursing.

IV

Aging in the Media and Other Places

This chapter will discuss selected content from the media, in particular, television, aging magazines, daily newspapers, and radio stations, as well as participant observation in other places.

I commenced my data collection with the media because it provided a prelude to the major themes of aging; and at this point, I was still undecided as to where to locate my more concentrated work. I started out viewing television programs in whatever context they were available to me. I was not selective. I perused the current television guides, and adjusted my video recorder to tape the programs. Needless to say this provided some data.

In the following pages I will summarize selected excerpts from this data, which I believe identify major themes of aging. I will begin with a program presented by Sally Jesse Raphael, namely: "I've become my mother's mother." This program portrayed role reversal of adult children, especially daughters caring for aging parents. It described the demands placed on the daughters and their families, and the dilemma involved in this process.

Several months later a similar type of program surfaced. This presentation was also by Sally Jesse Raphael and depicted grandparents as parents. This was a different kind of role reversal, where grandparents were raising their children's children, because the parents were absent (e.g., drug addiction or abandonment). Many of these grandparents were seeking to adopt these grandchildren. One grandfather on the program reported, "My birth certificate says 74, but

I feel 23." These people have formed a group named "Parents the Second Time Around" and are currently lobbying for legislation to get some of the drug money confiscated during drug raids to support these children.

Some time ago the media was brimming with news about Nelson Mandela's release from prison in South Africa. The event was vividly depicted whenever one turned on the television. The morning of his release an associate of his gave the following account of him: Mandela reveals that when he was a child "he envied his elders, their nice grey hair;" now that he is "71 and grey himself, he doesn't like it." The afternoon of his release from prison, he was described by media reporters as a lean, white haired, dignified, aging gentleman. A local newspaper ("Mandella Image," 1990) portrayed him as someone who speaks softly but leads with enormous power. This man of 71 years is categorized as aging; yet he is an image to young and old in South Africa. This man was locked away for almost 28 years. Today he is hailed as the most famous person in South Africa, yet prior to his release only a handful of people knew what he looked like. Archbishop Desmond Tutu described this man as "The symbol of our people" (p. 10). There is a mythology surrounding him that makes it almost impossible to separate the man from the idol. Was his invisibility part of the mystique, or is it the image of a 71 year old gray haired, dignified gentleman?

A television program on NBC interviewed Warren Littlefield the Executive Vice-President of prime-time programming. He stated that NBC and its counterparts on other networks are crediting actors and actresses fifty-something, and sixty-something, with joining today's rating winners. Persons such as Angela Lansbury, of *Murder She Wrote*, was consistently in the top 10 of CBS; and NBC was number one thanks to *The Golden Girls, Matlock, In the Heat of the Night*, and Robert Stack in *Unsolved Mysteries*. Robert Stack was described as portraying a father image and a comfortable image of an adult. It was reported that Stack, like others, could easily coast into retirement, but he recoils at even the suggestion. He stated, "To be retired is to be dead, when you are retired it means nobody wants you to work for them." Stack believes the audience likes to watch someone who has lived long enough to know what he is talking about.

It was recounted that when *The Golden Girls* first aired on NBC television, many critics believed that a comedy revolving around four senior citizens would not survive. They didn't count on the show's sense of humor, or the chemistry between the cast. It is believed that *The Golden Girls* bashes some of the stereotypes about aging, and dispels the myth for commercial sponsors that older actors and actresses only attract an older audience. Rather, *The Golden Girls* attracted more teens, children, and young people than many other shows. In addition, it got some of the warmest fan mail. In essence, the key is not how old the actor or actress is, but whether you have great roles for them to play. Networks also like to hire aging actors and actresses because of their image and because they lend authority and credibility to the show.

An article from *Catholic New York*, titled "Toddlers and Senior Citizens Hit it Off in Schervier Program" (Poust, p. 20), discussed an intergenerational program at a local nursing home. It reported that the "two most vulnerable segments of the population are the very young and the old" (p. 20). In this account, the nursing home had cared for one of these groups for many years, the older population. Since the opening of a day-care center it is now caring for the other group. The program is both formal and informal. One day each week the children visit the nursing home and sing songs or share an art project; informally the children mix with the aging patients and "bask in their affection" (p. 20).

The article described this encounter as providing the children "with warmth and comfort that only an aging person can give" (p. 20). In return, the aging people are recounted as becoming vitalized and animated when the young children arrive. The following accounts were given: tired eyes light up and expressionless faces break into smiles. One gentleman was reported as being especially touched by the children's presence. "He'd kind of gone into a shell and he didn't talk to anybody" (p. 21). When the children started coming he came out of his shell, he let the children sit on his lap, and now he talks to everybody (Poust, 1990). According to Kelly (1958),

> Loneliness has been aptly termed the curse of the aged. Some old
> persons sink into a kind of stupor and watch hopelessly as their close

friends die, one by one. Because they have made no effort to
cultivate new friendships, they soon are walled in by loneliness.
(Kelly, p. 150)

Mead (1975) tells us that contact between generations is healthy,
but it has been lost in the desperate helter-skelter of the post World
War II world. An article in *New Choices*, by Coles (1989) titled "On
Feeling Invisible," compared society's treatment of people past 70—
the stereotypes and the subtle rejections—with similar treatment of
blacks in Ellison's *Invisible Man*. One specific example the author gave
was the account of a 70 year-old woman, a board member of a
prominent cultural institution, whose suggestions are respected and
utilized where she is known, but in other situations is completely left
out. This is especially evident in department stores and restaurants,
where young people get preferential treatment. The author reminded us
that:

> Our social class and occupational status can affect our vision: we pay
> attention to people who talk and dress in ways familiar and
> comfortable to us, and we look away from others whose speech and
> appearance we have learned not to like. (Coles, p. 3)

An editorial in *Modern Maturity* by Betty Friedan (1989)
described America as being obsessed by youth for too many years. She
went on to say that age has been defined as a decline from a peak of
youth (male youth), "Age is denied, a fate worse than death" (p. 71).
She believes that the negative stereotypes of aging people are
reinforced by the media. Generally their examples of people over 60
years doing anything active, or dynamic, in the society is meager. She
explained that the reality of the situation is that many people over 60
are breaking down the stereotypes and defining a life for themselves
that affirms a fountain of age, rather than seeking the fountain of youth.
The author, who is 68 years old, breaks the stereotype: She is a visiting
professor at a university, a grandmother, and currently writing a book
on the "Fountain of Age."

As I continue my accounts of aging people, a newspaper article by
McWhirter, (1990) on an 80 year-old man is significant. This

gentleman was required to retire from his position as Vice-President in charge of minority-affairs at a large company, yet he continued to work as a consultant for the company. He describes retirement "as the blossoming of his new crusade," (McWhirter, 1990, p. 7), that is, teaching America's youth about business through a program he created, called "Learn and Earn." In addition, he spends time at his church working with high school students in Bible Study. He is quoted as saying, "I don't know anymore pleasure than coming here and getting something accomplished" (Mcwhirter, 1990, p. 7). He was voted man of the year by *Excel Magazine* in 1986. In 1987, Harvard University presented him with a distinguished service award. He was professor of business at Howard University for 30 years and the list goes on. This 80 year-old man was hailed as one of black America's Corporate Role Models, "the Jackie Robinson of business" (McWhirter, 1990, p. 7).

One point is clear—the media is full of success stories of people who are above 65 years. Some examples are: A man in his late 70s, who left office after serving two terms as President of the United States; a successor who celebrated his 65th birthday; while he was President. A Presidential candidate in his early seventies, and a Pope who maintains an active public life in his late seventies. A recent radio broadcast portrayed a 66 year-old grandmother arrested for operating a house of prostitution. An 87 year old Senator announced his intention to seek another term.

Television and other communication items also focus on health. The woes of animal fats and cholesterol seem to be a common thread, especially for people over 50 years. Television has many commercials for health products which affect the state of the individual. For instance, Angela Lansbury's commercial for Bufferin uses aches and pains as a given when you get older; but the discomfort is easily remedied by taking some Bufferin. Television fiction shows related to health and staying healthy generate emergency types of situations with quick remedies. On the research side, one can read longitudinal studies circulated by the National Institute on Aging if one wants to understand the aging process.

In the preceding accounts, the media described age-grading. A specific example of this was the account of the Schervier program. The documentary was presented in a positive fashion where opposite ends of the age spectrum were identified with their contributions to each other. Essentially, when both groups were allowed to integrate informally, nature took over. My question was, why was this such a wonder! Babies and children in general, have been basking and growing from the love and care of grandparents for years. The description of the event included an aging gentleman "who had gone into a shell and didn't talk to anybody" (Catholic New York, 1990, p. 21). The story explains the children's positive effect on him. While I would not negate the children's affect, my question is: was the gentleman lonely? Is this a part of aging? Did his age produce the catatonic state? Is it a negative aspect of aging? If it is, what about the rest of the residents? Is it a condition of institutionalization? Finally did his condition relate to the category of aging? Or was he a victim of cultural patterning? It seems to me, when the boundaries of aging in this institution were abolished, the human aspect took over.

Age-grading in the form of role reversal was evident in both programs presented by Sally Jesse Raphael, as well as dependence when health impairment transpires. In the first situation it was biological health, and the second scenario portrayed emotional health. The role of the family was also implicit in both cases. What the daughters are saying here is: When ill-health and the frailties of aging prevail, their mothers become dependent on them and they must care for them. Needless to say, this impinges on their personal and family life.

Likewise, the grandparents in the second scenario play a different type of role-reversal. Here, there seems to be enjoyment of the imposed role, as described by the grandfather. It seems to give him renewed life and the variable of economic resources surfaces.

Age-grading was also purported in the story of the 70 year-old board member. Again, one has the temptation to ask, Are the discriminatory rejections she describes related to a cultural code or her age? I agree with Coles that people have a tendency to gravitate to people who talk, dress, and act, in ways similar to ourselves. Perhaps a similar analogy would be ethnic groups living in their own area. We feel secure with sameness. Is it possible that the key was difference, not aging?

Another editorial in *Modern Maturity* talked about America's obsession with youth and the stereotypes of older people, including their passive role in society. The author blames the media for personifying these myths, and claims the reality of the situation is that people over 65 are breaking the stereotypes. She described seeking a fountain of age rather than a fountain of youth. The author, a woman of 68 years, described her own endeavors. The emphasis was placed on her being 68 years old; but if we temporarily erase the age, we have an energetic aging woman, who is a college professor and a grandmother. Are we talking about a person, or a stereotype, or a 68 year old woman? I believe we have an aging individual, demonstrating an active, independent life.

If this woman were 40 years old, would her contributions be significant? I believe so; I also believe 65 is used by society as a cultural marker for aging and it is just that, a marker. Much of the media data cited attests to this, as well as portraying the themes of keeping active and remaining independent.

It was noted that health on television is generated in emergency type situations with quick solutions. Yet, most of the illness that the aging actors would try to prevent would be chronic illnesses. The literature corroborates this. The media does not portray Doctor Kildare or the medical team of General Hospital making rounds in a nursing home. Perhaps this is representative of society in general; if we forget about it, perhaps it will go away.

This concludes the section on the media, which helped me to identify many major themes. I would now like to turn to some information I gathered through participant observation in other places.

PARTICIPANT OBSERVATION

In this section of the chapter, I will summarize information I obtained from participant observation in various places. While my search was by no means exhaustive, the findings did help me focus.

My first location was an airport. I chose this area because it provided a diverse group of people to observe. I made a particular point of being present during arriving and departing flights. There is an airline policy that people traveling with children, disabled persons, and aging persons, have priority when embarking on a departing airplane. An interesting pattern I observed was that when the flight attendants announced the flight's departure, the number of people in these categories grew. When the flights arrived, it seemed many people required wheelchairs. Airline employees collected their luggage and wheeled them all around the airport; yet many of these people walked steadily when leaving the airport. By contrast, others barely able to walk refused help.

In my community, Wednesday is "Senior Citizen Day." This means a 10% discount on all items for those who present a senior citizen card. I observed while shopping that some people bought a few items for themselves and presented their cards, but in many other instances young people bought many items, and grandma checked them out at the register, presented her card, and received the discount.

I also sat in a local fast-food restaurant during lunch time, in Yonkers, New York, and in St. Martin in the Caribbean. I wanted to observe the dynamics of the actors doing a common cultural trait— eating. What I observed was people of all ages ordering similar types of foods. Young people behind the counters scurried around to fill their orders. In general, the cultural dynamics in Yonkers was quite similar to St. Martin. People arrived for lunch with children and small babies. Some carried trays, others had take-out orders packaged in paper bags. Several men and women using canes as walking aides, ordered food to take out, and then sat at a table to eat. I assumed this was a more convenient way to carry food as it is a self service restaurant. Some people sat down and ate, others sat in groups and chatted and laughed as they ate. I did not observe any deference to any age group.

I noticed an interesting symbol in the Yonkers restaurant. A gentleman using a cane came to the counter to order; when the waitress gave him his food, he paid her, and then tipped his hat to her and smiled. After he walked away, the waitress laughed and remarked to her peers, "I wonder what that meant."

My final observation took place in St. Martin. The scene was an average restaurant located on the beach in one of the resort areas. The patrons were seated at tables for two, or in large groups. There was one exception—a white-haired, pleasant-looking male, approximately 70 years of age, who was seated by himself at a single table. What was interesting was that he did not seem the least bit lonely or uncomfortable. He chatted and laughed with the waiters and waitresses as he ordered a large meal. He also engaged in conversation with two women at an adjacent table. When a young child knocked over an ice-bucket which contained a bottle of wine, it created some confusion as to the best way to wipe it up. The gentleman calmly directed the staff and they followed his advice. I later saw the same gentleman in the Casino. Again he was solo, but he continued to have a great time, talking to others in a friendly outgoing manner. What made this gentleman so engaging? Was it his age, his personality, or was he just a warm friendly human being, whose affable approach was catching?

In the discussion just described, it was possible to learn only one thing. In these situations the aging actors used the stereotypes practically. According to Schultz (1962), the actors and society in general are operating under an "already organized world" (p. 30).

This concludes the section on participant observation. I will now turn to a discussion of an important aspect of the research—the settings.

NOTES

Blacks rejoice, South Africa: A new era. (1990, February). *Gannett Westchester Newspapers,* p. 10.

Coles, R. (1989, March). On feeling invisible. *New Choices,* 93-95.

Friedan, B. (1989, April-May). Not for women only. *Modern Maturity,* 66-71.

Kelly, G.A. (1958).*The Catholic marriage manual.*New York: Random House.

McWhirter, J., (1990, February 11). D.G. Fitzhugh *Gannett Westchester Newspaper.* pp.1,7.

Mead, M. (1975). *Blackberry winter: My earlier years.* New York: Pocket Book Edition.

Poust, J. (1990, February 8). "Look at all the grandmas" toddlers and senior citizens hit it off in Schervier Program. *Gannett Westchester Newspapers.* pp.20-21.

Schultz, A. (1962). Rules as explanations of action. In D.L. Wieder (Ed.), *Language and social reality.* The Hague, Netherlands: Mouton and Co.

V

The Language Of Aging

In this chapter I am going to look at discussions that I collected in several settings. Since my data spanned many areas of information gathering, I had difficulty deciding which of the many sources were most relevant to my study. I knew I had to streamline the presentation of my information, as well as choose the most relevant areas. I decided on five settings where conversations took place. Each setting imposed its own interests and agenda. In the following pages I will describe and discuss this language.

The first setting is a meeting with a group of friends sharing a holiday dinner in a home. I selected this setting because it included age conversation in a social gathering from a diverse group of people, including: an accountant, a nurse, an aging widow, a computer programmer, a bank manager, and a mechanic, among others. The informants will be described in more detail in the social organization chart. This was a multi-ethnic and inter-generational group. Since my study has to do with dialogue on aging, this social encounter provided relevant conversation for my research.

The second setting is conversation with an 83 year-old woman who lives alone at home. She relocated to her current apartment after her husband's death. The objective of the move was to live near her daughter. This interview provided aging dialogue from still a different stance than the preceding setting.

The third setting is dialogue with a 92 year-old woman who currently maintains her own apartment. This interview provided aging conversation from a different point of view, revealing a different life-style, different behaviors, and attitudes.

The fourth setting is age-talk in an Adult Community Residence. Since it is a place where elderly individuals live, I was interested in how the respondents would talk about their life-style and aging.

The fifth setting is an interview about a daughter's dilemma related to a family decision to admit her father to a nursing home. This interview produced talk about aging from a very different perspective, that is, age talk within a family.

I will now turn to a description of the settings, and a discussion of the talk.

AT HOME WITH A GROUP OF FRIENDS

The hosts were a young couple named Judy and Frank, of Irish and Greek ethnic origin, respectively. They will be described in more detail in the social organization chart.

The Physical Structure

This was the first time the young couple entertained in their new town house. It was a two-story dwelling clustered among several hundred other buildings in a suburban setting in northern New Jersey. As I entered this community, I was struck by the tall oak and elm trees that framed the grounds. There was evidence of new grass peaking through the neatly manicured lawns. Spring crocuses were already gracing the flower beds.

The community is situated on 30 acres of land. The buildings are two-story attached structures, designed to resemble houses rather than apartments. Each building has its own physically demarcated lawn. They are constructed of shingle, and every other townhouse is decorated with brick. Likewise, there is a variation in the color of the front door of each building. Centrally located to groups of houses is a swimming pool and a recreation building. There were adequate facilities available for guest parking. As I walked to my respondents building, I noticed several people walking their dogs.

The Social Context

I climbed the four concrete steps to the front door and rang the bell. I was greeted by Judy and Frank, who welcomed me warmly—Judy, kissing me on one cheek and Frank kissing me on both cheeks. When I smiled at him questionably and exclaimed "two kisses", he told me it was a family tradition, probably dating back to a Greco-European custom. We walked through a small foyer to the living room. There was a hub of conversation from the guests that were present. Frank introduced me, and explained simply that I was the researcher he had previously described. Their response was friendly and enthusiastic.

People chatted amicably. The television in the background vividly displayed the season's ball game and this seemed to be a major topic of male conversation. Some of the women joined the conversation; others chatted about shopping, work, children, and the season's festivities. The children interacted with all individuals, played independently in a corner of the living room, and re-arranged closets in other rooms, yet the hosts seemed unruffled by any of this.

This was a social event to celebrate the Easter holiday and it was marked symbolically. The men were wearing shirts and neckties. The women were dressed in fancy dresses and high heeled shoes. The children wore Easter outfits.

As I gazed around the living room, I noticed it had an air of warmth and coziness. There were light beige walls, melon drapes, a brown sofa and several comfortable chairs. There was a large coffee table in the middle of the room, made of glass, but resembling a piano. This was described by the hosts as their pride and joy. Several plants draped the table, such as an Easter lily, an azalea plant and a pot of tulips. These were gifts from the guests and served as a reminder of the feast of Easter. They were described by the hostess as "Easter decorations and a symbol of the onset of spring."

Getting Acquainted

The guests were invited to a buffet supper. The food was arranged on a table, decorated with a tablecloth of blue motif. Stack tables were strategically positioned for the people's comfort and availability of snacks and drinks. This set-up provided me with the opportunity to chat individually with the guests. People ate, drank, and socialized for about three hours, then the taping took place. Earlier, my hosts had prepared the guests for the discussion by informing them that I was conducting a study, and my research topic was "Aging."

Preliminary Events

Before describing the activities of the interview, I would like to point out that I was physically present in the living room during the entire evening. I asked Judy to initiate the conversation, because I wanted to remain as inconspicuous as possible. I believed this would add to the spontaneity of the conversation. While my focus was issues on aging, I wanted the discussion to be open-ended. I also wanted to observe behavior and interactions during the conversation.

Prior to the beginning of the conversation, I placed my Marantz tape recorder under a small padded stool in the corner of the room. My purpose in taping the conversation was to permit my full concentration on the interaction process, without the distraction of taking notes.

The guests were seated in a circle in the living room. Initial small talk included: Shall I turn the television off? Can I please have a drink first? Then there was the nervous joking and laughing as a prelude to the interview. I had given Judy some suggestions for opening the interview, which included: What is aging? When does aging begin? Who should take care of aging people? What about their health? Do you think aging people are treated fairly? How long should people be allowed to work? Is there a generation gap? One respondent asked me if the conversation should proceed in an orderly fashion. I informed him that they could talk in any order they chose, and that I preferred the conversation to be spontaneous.

What ensued was a combination of spontaneity, joking, laughter, serious talk, and it ended in a friendly fight. They quickly responded to Judy's questions and created their own talk. I said very little. The conversation progressed for over an hour. After I listened to the tape several times, I decided that the first 10 minutes of the conversation was most relevant to my research. I chose this segment because my interest lay in finding those moments where aging themes predominated. The following pages will depict this conversation.

THE SOCIAL ORGANIZATION OF
THE GROUP OF FRIENDS

Judy Tsolias:	Supervisor of cost accounting; 25; Bachelor's Degree in Social Work; Master's in Business Administration; "Irish"; wife of Frank Tsolias.
Frank Tsolias:	Public accountant; 26; Bachelor's Degree in Accounting; "Greek"; husband of Judy Tsolias.
Joseph Hontz:	Insurance analyst; 28; Bachelor's Degree in Management; "German"; husband of Barbara Hontz.
Barbara Hontz:	Bank manager; 27; "Italian"; eight months pregnant with her first child; wife of Joseph Hontz.
Donna Polinski:	Registered nurse; 27; Master's Degree in Nursing; "Irish"; mother of two children; wife of Buddy Polinski.
Buddy Polinski:	Computer programmer; 30; Bachelor's Degree in Computing; "Polish"; father of two children; husband of Donna Polinski.
Jim Nolan:	Controller; 50; Master's Degree in Finance; "Irish"; father of Judy; divorced.
Paul Photopulos:	Mechanic; 32; "Greek"; bachelor.
Helen Williams:	Part-time coordinator of lunch program in senior citizens center; 48; "German"; widow; daughter of Agnes Haum.
Agnes Haum:	"Grandma"; retired; 90 years; "German"; mother of Helen Williams; widow.
Kristan Polinski:	Five years; daughter of Donna and Buddy.
Dawn Polinski:	Two years; daughter of Donna and Buddy.

*Note: Quotation marks for ethnicity, express the fact that the individual when asked claimed membership in this ethnic category.

THE TALK

Judy sat in the center of the circle of friends and posed the following question: What is aging? I was sitting in the circle observing the respondents reaction and anxiously waiting for a response. Many looked surprised. I wondered if this was a different question than they had anticipated? After what seemed a long time, Buddy responded. I glanced at my watch, only 10 seconds had passed.

Buddy: Aging is good.

Donna: (looking animated) Why is it good?

Buddy: It's good! If I didn't get older I wouldn't have a child. If I was still a kid I wouldn't have a baby, so I age and I have a child, and I grow up with them.

(After Buddy made this statement his little two year-old daughter came running to him—calling daddy, she hugged him and he kissed her.)

(I believe the sincerity of his aging statement was communicated here).

(Buddy paused, then Judy pursued the conversation with another question.)

Judy: And when do you think aging begins?

(Again Buddy responded.)

Buddy: Everyday.

(At this time the room was quiet. People looked intent. Joseph was smiling, he responded.)

Joseph: After you get married.

(Everybody laughs.)

(Frank responds.)

Frank: Joseph, you hit that right on the head.

(Joseph continues.)

Joseph: You age in progression, you acquire more knowledge when you mature.

(Judy pursues the question.)

Judy: When does it start?

(Donna laughs, then she responds.)

Donna: Joseph doesn't know yet.

(Joseph laughs, everybody laughs.)

(Joseph responds.)

Joseph: I don't know I'm still in the stupid stage, I'm working my way to maturity.

(Laughter continues, then there was an immediate shift in the conversation by Donna. She directed a specific question to Helen.)

Donna: You work in a nutrition center how is it?

(Helen hesitates briefly then responds.)

Helen: Sometimes it's nice, when the people are nice. Some old people are nasty.

(Judy immediately picks up on this.)

Judy: What do they do that makes them nasty.

Helen: They complain that the food is not good. It's cold. It doesn't taste good.

(Judy nodded, then she shifted the conversation, this time to (Agnes)—"Grandma.")

Judy: Grandma! What do you think of old people?

Grandma: I hate them.

(Everyone laughed, and applauded Grandma. Then Judy's face became quite serious as she looked at Grandma and asked:)

Judy: Why Grandma?

(But before Grandma could answer Joseph responded.)

Joseph: Because she doesn't consider herself to be old.

(Then Grandma responds—smiling.)

Grandma: I'm not one of them.

(Joseph—smiling, responds.)

Joseph: See that.

(Grandma is still smiling, and looking pleased as she responds.)

Grandma: I'm only a young girl!

Judy: Grandma! How old do you have to be to be considered old?

(At this point everyone is laughing including Grandma, as she responds.)

Grandma: About one hundred and fifty.

(At this point there was laughter and some of the respondents began talking among themselves.)

I requested that they share their comments with the group. There was immediate cooperation, as Judy posed the following question:

Judy: What do you think about aging people health-wise as they get older?

(Donna immediately responded.)

Donna: I think it's very sad, they spend all their money on medications and health expenses.

(Grandma interjects.)

Grandma: And on vacations.

(This response seemed to spark Jim's interest, and he responded.)

Jim: Nothing wrong with vacations.

Judy: (Directing her question to Donna.) Do you think all the medications they take are necessary?

Donna: A lot of them are over medicated.

Judy: And they pay a lot of money for this!

Donna: And they pay a lot of money before they get anything back.

Judy: Isn't a percentage picked up by Medicare?

Donna: I don't know exactly. I think a certain percentage is picked up but it still has a deductible.

Judy: Do you think Medicare should pay a 100%?

Donna: Somebody should.

(For a while it seemed like the conversation was just between Judy and Donna, however I noticed the group seemed engrossed in the conversation. Then Joseph responded.)

Joseph: No! I don't think Medicare should pay a 100%. The individual should be liable for some of it. It's different if they have a catastrophic illness that could wipe them out. You should have to pay your own way for check-ups and medications.

(Donna responded again.)

Donna: (Angrily) Do you know what medication costs for a month?

(Grandma, tried to respond.)

Grandma: We hear America is the richest country. This country . . .
(she didn't finish her comment as Paul interrupted her.)

Paul: With Medicare if you can't afford it, the State picks up the bills.

Donna: There still has to be a better way.

(Joseph responds in a strong challenging voice.)

Joseph: Take Bob Hope you mean you're going to pick up the tab for his medication.

Donna: No! But he's not the bigger percentage of the population.

(I noticed that Frank sat pensive through the conversation, then he responded in an angry voice.)

Frank: But the nation is aging, people are getting older and older.

Donna: (persisting) Yes! But we have to do something better.

Joseph: Who's going to pay for it?

Donna: (Calmly) We are.

Frank: Where do you think the money will come from?

Grandma: From the people themselves.

Frank: (Turning to Grandma, in a gentler voice). Well that's the thing here. (Then Paul responds.)

Paul: It's the working people.

Buddy: What are old people going to do?

(Joseph responds).

Joseph: It's like Buddy said, we should provide for the people that need it, that need help. People like the Bob Hope's can take care of themselves.

CONFLICT AND CONCURRING THEMES

What was interesting here is that they discussed definitions of aging, laughed and joked about it, but they never did provide a definition; yet they continually negated the definition that was not there. So there was a definition by negation, but no definition of "When do you think aging begins?" There was a statement of everyday, which is not a particular time. Literally, this means a particular time was irrelevant; but it was also performed as a joke, the implication being that this was not to be taken at face value, that this was not what we expected to hear. Then there was a statement of "after you get married," and "when you mature" which put time into moments, denoting that moments are very important. But they make play moments, although they are not really play moments, because they are really important. So for approximately three minutes of the tape they discussed a definition of aging, which was from everyday to 150 years and all the possibilities in-between. But none was presented straightforwardly. All the answers are framed by laughter and jokes.

Then there was a movement to "they talk", that is, "They're nice when they don't complain about the food being cold," or "the food not tasting good." Then for several minutes health and the cost of medications was discussed. Again, there is "they talk" in the form of: "They pay a lot of money for medications." But nobody ever defined who they were.

Suddenly, there was a major shift in the conversation to Medicare and taxes for health care. The inference here was that aging also pertains to money, in the form of taxes, and the relationship within the family. Consider Donna's remark, "Somebody has to take care of them." Here it is expressed in paying taxes to support health care, including medications. But then it created a fight about who was going to pay for it, that is between the aging in general and the taxpayers. It was not personalized; it was not the grandmother in the room. Note the following statement from Joseph, "Because she doesn't consider herself old;" and Grandma's response, "I'm not one of them," again corroborated by Joseph, "See that." Everybody says Grandma does not fit the myth.

As stated previously, this was a 10 minute segment of the taped conversation. I taped for approximately 45 minutes, during which they continued to discuss taxes and aging. Then the conversation shifted to aging and retirement. The consensus felt that the age when a person retires should be an individual thing, depending on whether they can continue to perform their job appropriately. Most of the group felt people are better off being active. This theme was endorsed by Grandma, who reported that she worked for many years, and then found activities she enjoyed in retirement.

The concept of retirement led to a discussion on Social Security. People felt, as a culture, we are programming aging individuals to expect certain things. Social Security is seen as one of these expectations when one reaches the designated age. Then a discussion of "who will continue to pay for it" surfaced again. Most respondents felt people should be allowed to work when they are collecting benefits, without a penalty. Again this was discussed and argued at length. It was felt that allowing people to work would assist the funding of the Social Security treasury. Buddy compared retirement in Greece to the United States in the following statement, "In Greece and other countries if one wants to continue to work after retirement one can. In the United States, if someone collecting Social Security works, they are penalized for it".[1]

I turned the tape-recorder off after 45 minutes, yet the discussion continued after that, even during coffee and dessert. The discussion was lively and enthusiastic and some requested a copy of the tape. Yet during the whole process, aging was never defined. What started out to be a discussion on aging, turned out to be an event dominated by negating a definition of aging through jokes, and by talk about taxes, money, arguments, and a generalized they. What is interesting is that these people did not discuss the subject as the researcher expected. Aging was not discussed in terms of stereotypes or labels, but in an entirely different context. One can look at this discourse and analyze it in three stages: we know that aging has to do with definition, with money, as well as with the change in the relationship of the family, that is, "somebody has to take care of that person." So it relates to the family, and here the closest thing to taking care of the family is taxes; then it created a fight about who is going to pay for it, that is, between aging in general and the taxpayers in general.

NOTES

[1] Social Security benefits are withheld on a sliding scale when a beneficiary under 70 has earnings in excess of the annual exempt amount. Generally, the exempt amounts increase annually. For 1997, a beneficiary, 65-69 years can earn: $13,500, a beneficiary, under age 65, can earn: $8,640. S.S.A., 1997.

Social Security. (1997) Retirement earnings test exempt amounts, pp. 1-2.

VI

Dialogue with an 83 Year Old Woman

It was Saturday and I had gone to the shopping center to purchase a few items. I was in a department store trying on shoes and carefully evaluating how comfortable they were. A voice greeted me. It was a former patient of mine, Mrs. Doyle. I had met her several times in the shopping center before. She sat beside me while she waited for assistance. We exchanged polite conversation. I purchased my shoes and said good-bye to the woman.

About an hour later as I was walking to the parking garage, I met her again. We stopped to talk. During my conversation I mentioned my research on Aging. She was interested in what I was doing, and she volunteered to be interviewed. She gave me her phone number and suggested that I call her. She explained that the evening was the best time to find her home, and she thought this would probably be more convenient for both of us.

I called Mrs. Doyle about a week later. We made an appointment for the following Wednesday evening at 7:00. She gave me clear directions to her home, and informed me that it is difficult to park at that time of the evening. She told me the parking lot spaces are rented by tenants. However, she gave me the number of a space I could park in. She said it belonged to a friend who works evenings.

CULTURAL DESCRIPTIONS

I arrived at her place on a cool evening in October. She lives in a five-story apartment building in Westchester. The grounds were well lit and this displayed several well maintained lawns and shrubs. One could see some remnants of summer flowers, but there was a chill of fall in the air. There were two parking lots which were filled with cars. I was grateful to Mrs. Doyle for her thoughtfulness in arranging a parking space for me. I walked to the apartment building and rang her bell. As I waited for her to respond, two young boys came along and yelled into the intercom which opened the door. They laughed and went on their way. In the meantime, Mrs. Doyle rang back. I entered the building and started to walk towards the elevator, but since she lived on the second floor I changed my mind and decided to walk the stairs. By the time I reached the apartment, she was waiting for me at the door. We exchanged greetings and she invited me into her apartment. She ushered me into her living room.

She told me it was a three room apartment. Her living room was large and airy, but sparsely furnished. The furniture consisted of a couch and two love seats. An oriental rug covered the center of the floor. A round bamboo type cocktail table was placed in front of the couch. A television set was on and Dan Rather was reporting the evening news. She turned the television off. Sheer white curtains framed three large windows, and a pot of English ivy was placed on a table in front of the windows. The room was well lighted, and very neat and clean.

She said she had just made coffee and was hoping I would join her. We sat at the kitchen table drinking coffee. She also placed a plate of dietetic cookies on the table. I brought my tape recorder and a pad and pen which I placed on the table. I had obtained permission from her previously to use them.

Mrs. Doyle is a warm hospitable woman, who laughs easily. She exudes friendliness. She is relatively tall and slightly overweight. Her short white curls framed her round face. She wore a green dress.

As we sat at the table and drank coffee, we talked. She told me she has been a widow for 10 years, and has lived in this apartment for nine-and-a-half years. Her daughter located it for her after the death of her husband. She pointed to a picture of him on the refrigerator. She said he was only 71 when he died. They were living in Connecticut at the time. One night, they had been watching television, and he said he was tired, so he was "going to bed." Later when she decided to go to bed, she noticed the light was still on in the bedroom; when she spoke to him he did not respond. Eventually to her horror, she realized he was dead. Emotion filled her voice as she spoke.

Her husband had been a businessman all his life. During his career he had received many promotions. Because of this, they moved four times in 11 years. Finally at the age of 54, he and an associate decided to go into business together. It seemed to go well for about three years, then the pinch came. The business failed and they lost a lot of money. Most of it was money they had saved for their retirement. At 57 he had to go back to work for someone else in a lower paying position. He worked until he was 67 in order to recuperate some of the money he lost. She believed the whole venture broke his heart and caused his early death.

THE INTERVIEW

Up to this point I did not want to interrupt her, but I did want to interview her and either tape the conversation or take notes. I reiterated my request. Again she gave me her permission to do either. However, when I started to take notes, she mentioned that she was glad I chose that route. The interview began casually. I asked Mrs. Doyle how many daughters she had. She has one daughter, who is married and the mother of two children who are in their 30s. Again, I explained to her the purpose of my research.

I began with the following question:

Ethnographer: How would you describe yourself in terms of aging?

Mrs. Doyle: Somehow, I thought you would ask me about my health. I guess it's because I know you are a nurse.

I smiled and then reiterated my question.

Ethnographer: How would you describe yourself in terms of aging?

Mrs. Doyle: I'm 83 years old. I guess you would call me retired, but I was always a housewife.

Ethnographer: Would you call yourself middle-aged, young, aging, or
       how would you describe yourself?

Mrs. Doyle: Aging, but I don't feel old.

Ethnographer: What does aging mean to you?

Mrs. Doyle: I can't say, as I said I don't feel old myself. I feel good
       most of the time. I guess its when you can't walk, and you
       cannot help yourself.

I did not pursue the question any further as I did not want to
challenge her. Then I shifted the focus of the conversation.

Ethnographer: Would you say your life has changed drastically in
the last 10 years, in view of what you have just shared with me about
the death of your husband and moving to a new location.

Mrs. Doyle: Yes! Before I was very much a part of my husband's
life, you see I never worked. We had only one child, and after she
married we became closer as a couple. I still miss him very much, but
after I moved here I became closer to my daughter and grandchildren,
especially my grandchildren. Mrs. Doyle went on to tell me: That both
grand-children are married, and they each have two children. So that
makes her a great grandmother. At times she baby-sits for them, and
she really enjoys this. Her granddaughter married a man of the Jewish
faith, a musician. She said originally this posed a problem for her
because her family had always practiced the Catholic religion, and the
dual wedding ceremony troubled her. However she has grown to love
her grandson-in-law. Another added bonus is that their holidays are
celebrated at different times. So these young people are always present
at the major holiday celebrations. They don't have to take turns
spending the holidays with each family like her other grandson and his
wife.

Ethnographer: Do you see your grandchildren often?

Mrs. Doyle: Yes! Several times a month, they visit me, or I go to their
       place.

Ethnographer: How about your daughter, do you visit her often?

Mrs. Doyle: We get together about once a week. She volunteers at a
       local hospital and many times on her way home she stops to
       see me.

She continued to discuss her daughter and the fact that she never
worked and had always been a housewife. She married an attorney

after she graduated from college. She emphasized that she graduated from Smith college. I asked her if she was disappointed that her daughter never worked. Her answer was a definite, "No." She believed her daughter had a good life and always had time for her children. She informed me that her daughter is 58 years old now, and her husband is 60 and he is planning to go into semi-retirement. At this point I shifted the conversation and asked her how she would describe a day in her own life.

> Mrs. Doyle explained that she rises early, as she never was a good sleeper. She puts on the coffee and tests her blood sugar. As you know I'm a diabetic. She then prepares her breakfast, but first she gives herself an insulin injection. She drinks plenty of hot coffee with her breakfast. She loves coffee it's a free food, so she doesn't have to include it in her breakfast calories. Then she rests for a while and watches the morning news and a daytime program on television. This keeps her abreast of current events.

When asked about outside interests, she told me some days she goes to the senior citizen's nutrition center for lunch. That is if it accommodates her special diabetic diet, and she likes the particular food. Twice a week she attends exercise classes at the senior center. Other times she goes to the senior recreation center in the afternoon to play bingo and other games. She also takes the senior van once a week to do her shopping. She remarked, "The man is very nice, and always carries my packages to the door."

Sometimes she chats with her neighbors or has friends in for coffee. On Sunday she takes the mini-bus to church. She used to take a cab, but now the "Monsignor charters a bus and they pay a small fee." Some days she just sits in the house and reads the newspaper or watches television, and takes a nap in the afternoon. Sometimes she goes on the senior outings sponsored by the church. That is when she can afford it.

When asked about her health, her response was, "I feel fine as long as I test my blood sugar closely, take my insulin, and adhere to my diet." She visits her physician once a month. She also takes pills for her high blood pressure. She explained to me that she receives her health care at a local medical group that accepts her Medicare assignment and attends to all her health needs. "Medicare even paid for my glucometer for testing my blood sugar," she explained. She must take insulin each morning by injection. This was difficult at first, but now she is used to it. She was diagnosed as a diabetic shortly after moving to her apartment. She has also been hypertensive for 10 years. She described her medicine as expensive for someone who is on a fixed income, but she manages. I asked her where she learned how to administer her insulin injections. She said they taught her in the hospital. In addition they gave instructions to her daughter. I told them, "I wanted to take care of myself." After she left the hospital a visiting nurse used to come to her house to help her until she became more confident with giving her own injections.

As we talked the phone rang and it was a friend. She told her she had a guest and would call her back in the morning. I asked her how she would compare life when she was growing up with today's young people. In answer to my inquiry, she told me she grew up in New York City. She was one of five children, the second youngest in the family. Her parents were very strict. As teenagers they used to go ice-skating in the park, or to the movies, and then they all gathered at the local candy store. They usually had a curfew and they made sure they got home at the prescribed time. She met her husband at the candy store and married at 19. "Things were much simpler in those days," she stated. She believes today's youth have more stress, and its easier to get into trouble. She stressed, "I'm grateful my grandchildren turned out all right." She thought it was positive that so many people drive their own cars. She said, "I never drove a car myself and I'm sorry about that. I wished I had learned to drive when I was younger." She finished by saying "I'm too old to learn now."

At this time I shifted the focus of the conversation by asking her if she could describe how aging feels to her. The following will describe her response:

> Well it feels pretty good. I'm 83 years old. I feel good most of the time. I get around well. I can take care of myself. I guess my diabetes is caused by aging. They call it the mature kind. I guess this also

applies to my high blood pressure. I never had that until 10 years ago. But I still think I have many more good years left.

Ethnographer: How do other people of comparable age seem to you?

Mrs. Doyle: Some good, some bad. It's an individual thing. Some are in good health. Some of them think they are too old to do anything. Some are in homes.

Ethnographer: How do you perceive the role of people your age? What do you feel the expectations are?

Mrs. Doyle: I'm not sure, sometimes people think we are helpless. Some people treat you in a patronizing way, and some people are nice and respectful. Sometimes people laugh when they hear you go to exercise class. Others encourage you. I used to be a foster grandparent, I helped out in a grade school with two boys. I helped them with their reading. The people there really appreciated you, especially the children. The teachers said we had a lot to contribute. A friend of mine told me that when she started to use a cane it was a lot easier to cross the street. Cars would stop to let her cross and people offered to help her. I think some people don't realize we are healthy, intelligent, people.

Ethnographer: Could you anticipate your life changing much in the next five years or so?

Mrs. Doyle: No! I hope not. I'm mostly healthy and I try to take care of myself to keep it that way. I have friends and family. Sometimes I get lonely, but this is really because I miss my husband. I'd like to have a pet, a dog, but it would be too much to walk her in the cold weather, especially when there is ice on the ground.

She continued to explain that someone in her building who was walking a dog fell and broke her hip. When asked about a cat, she replied, "I don't like cats."

FAREWELL

We chatted for a few more minutes. I noted the time on her kitchen clock and it was almost 9:30. I mentioned that it was getting late, and perhaps she was tired of being interviewed. Her response was that she enjoyed it. Additionally, I was worried that her neighbor would be coming home from work and need her parking space. She offered me some soda before I left. Diet soda is all I have she told me. I thanked her but declined.

I thanked Mrs. Doyle for the interview and for participating in my research. Despite my objections, she insisted on walking me to the elevator. She said, "The exercise will be good for me." She ambulated in a steady confident fashion. I took the elevator to the ground floor and walked to my car.

DESCRIBING THE THEMES

Mrs. Doyle is a woman who is completely in charge of her life. The theme of independence is evident in the way she conducts the events of her daily living, takes responsibility for her own health problems, and by the way she handled the death of her husband. Independence is communicated in her talk about wanting to be able to administer her own insulin and not have to depend on her daughter. It is described in her accounts of getting to church, and in her fantasy of driving a car.

Independence is connected to health by the way she monitors her blood sugar, administers her own insulin, plans her own diabetic diet, takes her anti-hypertensive medication, and follows through on medical supervision. Health talk was clearly articulated as she discussed adhering to her diet at home and other places such as the nutrition center. Implementing the psychomotor skills of testing blood glucose, administering insulin, adhering to her diet, and exercising twice a week are ways of maintaining health. That is, "She feels fine," when she performs these rituals.

Money and health are clustered together in several different contexts. In discussing her husband, Mrs. Doyle discussed money, that is, the failure of the business caused her husband a broken heart and subsequent death. This issue also influenced the stability of their life. Most of the family savings had been lost in this business venture, and her husband had to work until he was 67 to remunerate the money he lost.

It is an issue for her health maintenance because if the health agency did not accept her Medicare assignment, paying her medical bills on her fixed income would be a dilemma. Again the issue of money was raised relative to her medication. It was described as expensive when one is on a fixed income. Yet the maintenance of her health depends on her taking her anti-hypertensive medicine. In regard to money there is some contradiction; Medicare is described as covering her medical expenses and buying her glucometer, yet she has to pay for her medicine which is difficult on a fixed income.

Activity is clearly linked to independence. It is demonstrated in the way she ambulates, in her social activities, her shopping activities, and in the implementation of her religious practices. It is connected to health relative to "doing exercises" and in her talk. For instance, when she walked me to the elevator she said, "The exercise is good for me." She also spoke of her regrets of never learning to drive a car. A car would have provided the independence of going places when she wanted to, without depending on buses, vans, cabs, and so on. Again, there is an element of dependence here. Mrs. Doyle functions in a world where she must depend on a time schedule of buses, vans, and cabs.

In her talk about family, Mrs. Doyle described her daughter finding an apartment for her after the death of her husband. This would provide the mother with closer proximity to her, rather than remaining at a distance in Connecticut. Yet she described herself as becoming closer to her grandchildren since she moved. The theme of family was implied when she spoke of family holidays with her grandchildren. Mead (1975) spoke to family in her statement, "Everyone needs to have access to both grandparents and grandchildren in order to be a full human being" (p. 311). Perhaps the family pattern interrupted by her husband's death is continued in her grandchildren, and this is a source of fulfillment for her. Again, Mead described, "The human unit of time as the space between a grandfather's memory of his own childhood and a grandson's knowledge of those memories as he heard about them"

(p. 311). However when she spoke of loneliness, it was addressed in the context of missing her husband.

Mrs. Doyle described contrasts in adherence to family values in her generation as opposed to current family mores. She described things as simpler in those days, and today's youth as having more stress. Yet what she described as stress may be a greater need to express independence. One significant link she identified was people driving their own cars, yet she described this as a positive facet of the culture. Her accounts of her always remaining a housewife and never seeking employment was viewed by her as a positive family contribution. Likewise her daughter getting married after college and never seeking a career is perceived as beneficial to the family unit. What she regards as beneficial may be a category of culture assigned to women before they became culturally absorbed in the career process.

Age-grading is frequently identified in this conversation. It was identified initially when Mrs. Doyle discussed her husband in the statement that he had to work until he was 67 years old. It appeared many times in the discourse in the form of categories such as old, senior citizen, young. It was connected with health when she described her diabetes as caused by age, "I have the mature kind." The inference here was that it is part of the territory that goes with aging. This concept was also inferred in her account of her high blood pressure. Yet she believes she has many more good years left. She sees age as an individual thing. Other people of comparable age to her were described as "some being in good health, others too old to do anything, and some in homes." There is a disparity in this concept of aging.

Despite the continuous dialogue of age-grading language, Mrs. Doyle would not describe herself in terms of age. She remarked that she does not feel old, in fact she feels good most of the time. Her supposition was that aging occurs when you cannot walk or help yourself. One could infer that aging to her meant dependence and inactivity.

The cultural values of religion, caring, loneliness, and friendship are also identified. While religion was not a central focus of Mrs. Doyle's life, it was seen as a cultural value. It was important to her in her granddaughters wedding. Marrying outside her own religion was seen as a problem and also a benefit. While she initially objected to the fact that her grandson-in-law was not a Catholic, she also saw it as a benefit on holidays when the whole family could be together, so there is a contradiction here.

Religion is also tied to independence. She traveled to church by cab, and currently by taking a van, provided by the Monsignor for a small fee. Here the mode of transportation was also tied with money. The van is an inexpensive ride as opposed to paying cab fare. This would be important to someone on a fixed income. Religion was discussed only as a cultural value as previously described. The talk did not include discussion of its process. Religious symbols such as pictures, statues, or votive lights were not displayed in her apartment.

Caring was communicated in her concern for her husband in his heartbreak over his failed business, and his extended period of employment to supplement his business losses. It was practiced in her role of foster grandparent, and in her statements about her great-grandchildren. It was apparent in her statement of visiting friends that "can't go outside anymore." It was even demonstrated in her interactions with myself, for example, when she arranged a parking space for me.

Loneliness was overtly described at one point when Mrs. Doyle spoke about missing her husband. Owning a dog was seen as a solution to ameliorate the problem. However, it was not possible to own a dog because this would create the problem of walking her, and this could lead to falling on the ice in the winter time. However, this loneliness was not connected to aging. It related to missing her husband. Additionally, the problems owning a dog would incur were not related to aging. Essentially, it would be a problem to walk him and you could fall as someone in her building did.

Friendship is something this respondent used in effecting a strategy to prevent loneliness. She is well connected to the people in her apartment house, to events at the senior center and the nutrition center. She watches television shows, Dan Rather and Opra Winfrey, and reads the newspapers to stay in touch with world events. She is a sociable person and interacts with friends. She goes shopping, even if only to window shop. She uses the senior citizen van to shop, which provides the additional bonus of being with other people.

Mrs. Doyle also interacts well with younger people. She has a close relationship with her grandchildren. This was expressed in her remark about her grandson-in-law, "I have grown to love him, and he is so good to me." She baby-sits for their children. It seems that the bonds between this woman and her grandchildren are extraordinarily rich ones.

What was interesting here is that there are four moments where age-grading talk took place. The concerns revolved around health, money, independence and family. Independence is important because as long as Mrs. Doyle is able to perform her insulin, diet, and medication activities she believes she can stay healthy. Here independence maps with health. However to maintain this health she must have medical care which is difficult to pay for if you are on a fixed income. The health care agency accepts her Medicare assignment, except for the expensive medication. This is where the issue of money was covertly raised. Activity is connected to independence because in order to perform all of the previously mentioned activities, one must be an active person. Additionally, activity is linked with staying healthy.

While family is an issue here, it was not mentioned in a similar context as the previous scenario. Here it was mentioned in the realm of getting the respondent an apartment closer to the family after the death of her husband. There could be an implication of dependence here, yet in the talk that I heard it was not mentioned. Family in this setting was related to friendship and family relationships. Here we have a different approach than the previous setting; here family was concerned with relationships, not with money or health.

Independence is important for Mrs. Doyle because it maps with health and activity, which compliment each other. Here we also have a different approach with money. It is used to prevent illness and maintain an ongoing health problem independently. However, it could be an issue, as she lives on a fixed income. Money relative to health care was also an issue in the preceding setting, albeit different circumstances. Here we have a person who has an elevated blood pressure regulated by medication, and diabetes, which she controls with exogenous insulin; yet she considers herself healthy as long as she can continue to perform these health functions.

Here the boundary language is not as clearly evident as we shall see in the following settings. Mrs. Doyle is currently independent, unless her quality of health deteriorates.

While there were many instances of age-grading in this conversation, the respondent did not provide a definition of aging. This was similar to the group of friends in the previous setting.

NOTES

Mead, M. (1975). *Blackberry winter: My earlier years.* New York: Pocket Book Edition.

VII

Dialogue with a 92 Year Old Woman

The next interview was with a 92 year-old woman named Mrs. Haverty. The interview took place in the woman's apartment, which is on the sixth floor of a cooperative apartment building in Westchester. I arrived for the interview at 11:00 on a Saturday morning. I had met Mrs. Haverty on several occasions before. Her daughter arranged the interview.

When I arrived at her apartment, I rang the door bell three times. This is the password, as she doesn't open the door to anyone. After a couple of minutes a voice asked, "Who is it?" She peered through the peep-hole in the door; when I identified myself she opened the door. She used a tripod cane for support. A nuisance she called it, "But slowly becoming a necessity." She was dressed in a pink floral housecoat. Her hair was light-grey colored and neatly combed. She wore pink-rimmed glasses. Her cheeks were a delicate pink, and she wore a pale pink colored lipstick. She looked more like a lady of 72 years than 92. She greeted me warmly and invited me into her studio apartment.

TOURING HER ISLAND

We first passed through her tiny kitchen. A small dinette table graced the center of the floor, and a bowl of colorful artificial flowers was placed in the center of the table; a square blue doily edged with white was placed under the flower bowl. I later learned that she crocheted the doily. To the right of the table was a sink and counter space; below the counter was a tiny refrigerator. I couldn't miss the wonderful aroma from the crockpot on the counter. "It's tenderloin," she told me, "I cook one every week. I used to cook it on the stove, but now my daughter worries that I may forget to turn off the gas. So I put the meat in this pot on low, and it can boil all day." She proceeded to tell me, "Initially I hated it, but now I find it very convenient." There was no window in the kitchen, but an exhaust fan over the stove compensated for this. A small china closet was placed against a cornered wall. On the other wall there was a small shelf, with a blue votive light. Over this hung a religious picture. "That light burns 24-hours a day," she told me.

She took me on a tour of her little castle. From the kitchen we walked through a small hallway to the bathroom. This was decorated with blue shower and window curtains, white walls, and an African violet plant on the window sill. "No more throw rugs on the floor," she said, "I have to keep my children happy. They're afraid I'll slip on the rugs." We then proceeded to the living room. On one corner was a bed, neatly fixed. "It's a convertible couch," she informed me, "But I find it too hard to fold up everyday, so now I decorate it with a nice spread. I think it looks fine." She seemed to be asking for my approval. On the other side of the room was a mantle-piece; the top was covered with family pictures. Adjacent to this was a small dining table with four chairs. Again, flowers were placed on the table. The floor was covered with red tweed carpet, which blended well with the red print drapes. Other furnishings included a comfortable looking rocking chair and a straight back chair, all strategically placed to provide optimum view of the television screen.

On the rocking chair lay a roll of pink and white yarn and a crochet needle. "It keeps me occupied," she told me. She insisted that I sit on the rocking chair, and offered me some coffee or tea. She acknowledged that her daughter had explained to her the purpose of my visit. She informed me that she was delighted to be able to assist in my study, but she worried that she would not do the interview the right way. I reinforced the purpose of my interview and managed to put her at ease. At this point I decided not to use my tape recorder, and I did not take notes in her presence, as I felt it would inhibit the spontaneity of the discourse.

THE DIALOGUE

The conversation centered around her activity. She shared with me that she is not as active as she used to be, and at times felt lonely because of this. "I generally find a way around this by walking around my apartment as this keeps me from getting stiff. I take the elevator down to the mail box, and I usually meet someone to talk to on my way. It's important to keep active," she told me. When the weather is warm, she sits out in the courtyard. During the long days of winter when the weather is cold, she spends time looking out the window to see people coming and going. She crochets a lot of table pieces which she uses as gifts for family and friends, and to decorate her apartment. She has a list of favorite television programs that she views daily. She loves to talk, and uses her telephone freely to talk to friends and family. She has one special friend that comes to visit weekly who keeps her informed about the people and the activities at the senior center. "I used to be an active member there," she told me.

She explained that it was difficult to get to Church on Sunday, yet her religion was important to her. As a solution, a young woman from her parish brings her Communion each Sunday, and she watches Mass on television. She said, "It was an adjustment at first, but I got used to it." She also likes to read, and sometimes has to use a magnifying glass for very small print. She subscribes to two weekly newspapers, and also reads the *Enquirer* weekly. "My grandson gave me the subscription for a Christmas present," she said. "At first I thought it would not interest me; but now I enjoy reading it." One of the weekly newspapers she reads is the *Irish Echo*. It "keeps me in touch with my heritage," she explained. As we talked about this, she pointed to a small painting on the wall. It was a small farmhouse, symbolic of the house she was raised in back in Ireland. She painted it herself. The idea grew out of some art lessons she took at the senior center when she first retired. She looked proud of her accomplishment, and then a little sad when she explained, "My hands are not steady enough to paint anymore."

As the conversation continued, she shared other aspects of her life. She looked wistful as she described her inability to walk out and shop independently like she used to. She acknowledged that the support of her children, grandchildren, and helpful neighbors remedied the situation. A family member does her food shopping each week, and neighbors pick up an item of food if need be. Other family members take her shopping frequently for incidentals, to the hairdresser and to family functions. "I get a little dizzy at times," she explained, "and am hesitant to travel too far alone." She does not take medication and described her physician as stating, "My recent blood pressure reading was as good as a young woman's." She expressed gratitude for her health, and a sufficient pension to live on. She misses having a pet around the house, especially a dog, but realizes it would be difficult to walk him and care for him adequately.

As the interview concluded, I thanked this delightful woman and exchanged farewells.

DISCOVERING THE THEMES

For Mrs. Haverty, aging talk is performed around articulated themes of keeping healthy and staying active. The theme of maintaining independence is also implied. It is central to the other themes.

The conversation produced other interesting cultural values, such as religion, family, loneliness, friendship, improvisation. Mrs. Haverty defined health as not taking medication, and having a "blood pressure reading as good as a young woman's." She spoke of getting a little dizzy at times, but did not relate this to health; instead she viewed it as a hindrance to traveling alone.

She organized her activity around cooking her own meals, taking care of her apartment, and walking around her apartment "to keep from getting stiff." Her ambulation is facilitated by using a tripod cane, described by her as "a nuisance but slowly becoming a necessity." These activities are seen by Mrs. Haverty as modalities for keeping active and maintaining independence.

Her social structure consists of family, friends, and neighbors; they are her connection to the world beyond her apartment. They do her shopping, take her to the hairdresser and family functions, and are available for other necessities if she needs them. Friends and neighbors are an outlet for conversation, and a solace for loneliness. Family is quite prominent in her talk, especially in the area of safety. This was evident by her comment about her daughter, "My daughter worries that I may forget to turn off the gas." She accommodated this worry by using an electric crock pot that cooks her tenderloin very slowly, instead of cooking on the gas stove. Another instance of family was displayed by her comment, "No more throw rugs on the bathroom floor. I have to keep my children happy, they're afraid I will slip on the rugs." There was almost a hint of secrecy here, or was it the American trait of conformism? Despite this subtle constraint, she exhibited coercive power on the part of the children regardless of their well meaning intentions. It was also indicative of Mrs. Haverty's limited independence. By comparison, family talk for Mrs. Doyle related to moving closer to her daughter, friendship and family relationships.

Mrs. Haverty circumvents her physiological impediments by improvisations, such as: embellishing her sofa bed with a decorative cover because she is unable to fold it into a couch; using a crock pot for cooking; exercising to prevent her from getting stiff; and crocheting to keep herself occupied, as well as providing a source of gifts for family and friends.

Her religious beliefs are oriented around the Catholic ideology. A central focus of her life, as expressed in her conversation, is watching mass on television and having someone bring Communion to her home. The symbols of her religion were displayed in the form of a votive light placed beneath a religious picture. The light burns "24-hours a day," she exclaimed. Religion is linked with the themes of health, independence, and activity, since Mrs. Haverty had to use her creativity to compensate for her physiological deficiencies. She hinted that she would rather attend religious services independently in her statement, "It was an adjustment at first . . . but I got used to it." She substituted a new pattern for an old one.

Loneliness and friendship are clustered together. They are expressed in statements of feeling lonely because she is not as active as she used to be. She remedies the loneliness by looking out the window to see people coming and going, sitting in the courtyard, talking on the telephone, weekly visits from a friend, having a friend keep her informed of the activities at the senior center, and meeting people on the elevator. She navigates loneliness with friendship, which overlaps with activity and independence.

What was interesting, is that you could analyze the talk in three stages. Mrs. Haverty maintains her activity and independence within her little island, albeit in a limited fashion. But she must depend on others beyond these boundaries to help her maintain this island. Unlike Mrs. Doyle in the preceding setting, Mrs. Haverty's boundaries are restricted to her apartment complex.

The realm of money was mentioned briefly by her when she remarked that she was grateful for having a sufficient pension to live on. It was not discussed in the same context in the first two settings. However, the dialogue did include family and intergeneration talk.

VIII
Aging in an Adult Community Residence

During the process of my data gathering, I visited an adult community residence. A resident must be 65 years or older, be in reasonably good health, and be able to perform all activities of daily living independently. I thought visiting such a residence would provide another aspect of the culture of aging. I visited the residence on a Saturday morning in June. The building was located high on top of a hill in a quiet suburban area. It was a red brick building approximately three stories tall. I was informed that it housed 200 residents, that is, 175 females, and 25 males. The building stood on several acres of lush green grass, spotted in several areas by round plots of multi-colored flowers. There was an aura of tranquillity as I walked to the front door of the building.

ENTERING

As I entered, I proceeded to the information desk on my left. I was directed to sit in the reception room until my guide arrived. This was a large room with several sofas and large comfortable looking arm chairs. Several hanging plants hung from planters on the walls. In addition, several swing lamps hung from the ceiling, thereby providing a well lit area. A television was positioned in the center of the floor. I sat in the reception room for approximately 15 minutes until my escort arrived. This gave me an opportunity to observe the residents. I noticed that most people used a cane of some type, and a few people used walkers. People were continually arriving and departing on the nearby elevator. Some people sat for a few minutes before progressing to their next activity. Some watched television, others stared into space, while still others conversed with each other.

SEEING THE SOCIAL STRUCTURE

I greeted several of them, and they responded politely, and then continued with their own agenda which seemed to be a process of moving on to the next activity. One woman sat next to me on the couch with her head leaning towards the floor. I greeted her and she responded weakly. She told me her name was Priscilla and that she was resting for a while before she went to the exercise program. I noticed she was breathing rapidly. She said she had recently been discharged from the third floor, and she wanted to keep her strength up through exercising. She told me she wanted to be able to stay in her own room on the second floor. She used a walker and complained of aches and pains in her joints. She was neatly dressed. She wore a two piece yellow dress, and dark rimmed glasses. I noticed a tiny hearing aid attached to her glass frame. Then my escort arrived, and I bade farewell to the woman.

My escort introduced herself as Anna. She said she was a resident of the institution who volunteers several hours per week of her time. She was a spry woman with dark brown hair and brown eyes, framed with large thick rimmed glasses. Her eyes had a gentle expression, and she was dressed neatly in a light green dress. As the conversation progressed, she told me she was 75 years old. She took me on a tour of the building, beginning with the first floor. We visited the dining room first. This was a bright airy room, with walls covered with yellow flowered wallpaper. Many tables were evenly spaced throughout the room. Each table was covered with a yellow table cloth, and a small vase of fresh carnations was placed in the center of each table. Six chairs surrounded each table. Anna explained that six is the limit at each table. This is planned to provide a more intimate and home-like atmosphere at mealtime. She described the food as good, and added that individual diets are planned carefully for a healthful effect.

We left the dining room and moved on to the activity room where an exercise class was in progress. Large numbers of women and a few men were participating. Keeping active is very important around here, Anna explained. The participants did not seem disturbed by our intrusion, so we watched the activities for a few minutes. Everybody was actively participating as one dark haired slim woman led the exercises. We left the exercise room and walked to the library. This was a cozy room with many shelves of books. Two long tables with chairs were placed in the center of the room. Soft music played in the background. Several women sat quietly reading.

As we left the library, Anna suggested we take the elevator to the second floor, where the residents suites were located. As we got off the elevator, I noticed the architectural lay-out of the floor was similar to the first floor. Adjacent to the elevator was a couch and several large comfortable chairs. In the center was a large round table with a vase of pink carnations. The walls were painted light blue, and the floors were covered with light blue carpet. Again, many plants hung from planters on the walls.

Several women sat on the couch conversing. We sat for a few minutes and talked with them. Other people were scurrying along the corridors to rooms, some using canes, others using walkers, and still others were moving along independently with a steady gait. Most of the doors to the residents suites were closed, so Anna took me on a tour of a vacant suite. It included one large room with a double bed covered with a rose colored bedspread. The room was adequately furnished with a night-stand, chair, and a lamp adjacent to the bed. The floor was covered with thick rose colored carpet. The room was L-shaped. It provided a small dining area, furnished with a small round grey table and two chairs. Again, flowers graced the center of the table. Off the dining area was a small kitchen, efficiently equipped with a refrigerator, stove, work-space and closets. The kitchen, Anna informed me, makes it convenient for preparing a snack or entertaining a guest. The kitchen overlooked a flower garden. All suites have a similar size and design, only the color scheme is different Anna said.

We left the suite and walked down the corridor. As we came to the end, Anna put her finger over her mouth, as if to whisper. "This is where the rich couple live she exclaimed." They have a suite with several rooms. It's beautiful. I visited them once." It seems the couple moved here from another state, so they would be near their son and his wife. It is reported, they really like the place, and they have their own personal housekeeper. While walking to the elevator, we looked out a window which overlooked a parking lot. Many cars were parked there. Anna pointed to a brown Chevrolet that belonged to her, and emphasized that the other cars belonged to residents also.

CROSSING THE BOUNDARIES

Finally we took the elevator to the third floor. I learned that this was the floor that the residents were sent to if they had a stroke or any type of debilitating illness. Generally, they were cared for and rehabilitated there when they returned from the hospital. It was an institutional policy to provide rehabilitation for healthful restorative measures for the residents. People on this floor were not required to go to the dining room for meals; the floor had policies geared to the physically disabled person. I noticed residents sat around in wheelchairs. Several staff members were in attendance. The television was playing loudly, and the air of independence was missing. I spoke with some residents and they responded feebly. Most of them were anxious to return to the second floor. We left the third floor and walked to the elevator. Before we reached our destination, we made one more stop at the Chapel. This was a small cozy room, with plain wood seating, and a center aisle covered with green carpeting. There was a small wooden altar. Placed on the altar was a book stand with a large book, and a single candle glowed in front of the altar.

This was the end of my tour. Before I left, I felt compelled to ask the question, Why do people like to come to an adult residence? The ambiance was great, I could not deny, but what else? Anna shared her reasons and she said they were pretty representative of most people.

VERBAL INTERACTION

I would like to summarize the responses of Anna's story:

Ethnographer: Why did you come to live in this residence?

Anna: I didn't want to live alone.

Ethnographer: You never lived alone before?

Anna: Well yes! But I had retired and I wanted to stay healthy. They look after you here, and you have someone to talk to. There are always people around and something to do.

Ethnographer: You like it here?

Anna: I love it. I can take a ride in my car when I feel like getting away from the place.

Ethnographer: Are the other people friendly?

Anna: Yes! I have lots of friends. My only complaint is that there are not enough men, and some of the ones that are here are married.

Ethnographer: Can you tell me about the third floor?

Anna: Well nobody wants to go there because its the disabled floor. People usually need help when they go up there.

Ethnographer: How long do they stay there?

Anna: Only until they are feeling well again, can help themselves, walk alone with a cane or walker, and eat in the dining room.

Ethnographer: Does everybody come back to their original suite?

Anna: Yes! Except for a few people who are too disabled to leave the third floor.

Ethnographer: I notice a lot of people use canes and walkers here.

Anna: Yes! They suggest you do, if you have any unsteadiness walking.

Ethnographer: Does everybody on the second floor eat in the dining room?

Anna: Yes. You must. They will only bring you a tray in your room if you have the flu or something.

I said good-bye to Anna and left the building. As I walked to my car I reflected on the people I met, our conversations, and the cultural themes that organize life in an adult community residence. Obviously the residents had adapted to the cultural norms and regulations that made living in this institution possible. Albeit, some of the regulations were subtly implemented. In considering this, one thinks of the residents using canes and walkers if they were in anyway unsteady on their feet. Looking at it another way: this subtle cultural regulation provided a method of preventing falls. Did the cultural patterns in the institution help the residents to maintain a healthy life-style? For example, much of the residents talk pertained to staying healthy, keeping active in order to stay away from the third floor. There were also the symbols of walkers and canes in this community.

CONNECTING THE THEMES

Age-grading permeates this community residence. It begins with requirements for admission: a prospective resident must be 65 years or older, be in reasonable good health, and be able to perform all activities of daily living independently.

Activity talk dominated this visit, both in overt usage of the term and as a link for other categories connected to it. The cluster of themes included staying active, staying healthy, and remaining independent. The dialogue also produced other cultural values of privacy, wealth, and fellowship.

Staying active is expressed through a variety of cultural symbols; for instance, when one enters the reception room one is greeted by residents using canes and walkers, resting for a few minutes, and then proceeding to the next activity. People are continually arriving and departing on the elevator. Institutional policy supports the concept of activity by providing exercise classes. The necessity of keeping active was described by Anna as "very important." Staying active maps with remaining independent and staying healthy. These attributes are important because if a resident stays healthy and active, she remains independent, and stays within the boundaries of the second floor.

This is the significance of the themes. For instance, if a resident suffers a debilitating illness, such as a stroke, or falls and breaks a hip, he or she will be unable to use a walker or a cane, and will then have to cross the boundary to the third floor. Even though a resident may be lucid and mentally competent, his or her independence is limited, and activity will be restricted to bedrest or a wheelchair. Peers will also have limitations in mobility and independence. As stated by Anna,

"Nobody wants to go there." It's the disabled floor and people usually need help when they go up there.

This concept was also expressed by Priscilla, who was recently discharged from the third floor. My personal assessment of her revealed an aging individual, slight of stature with rapid respirations, yet motivated to continue her journey to the exercise room after she rested. She had two objectives—relief of her aches and pains, and a desire to increase her strength through activity which, in turn, would maintain her health and independence. She informed me that she had just returned to the second floor after recuperating from a fractured hip. She had no desire to go back to the third floor.

Staying healthy was also a reason given by Anna for coming to the residence. This was also a focus of the institution, promoted by carefully planned diets, good food, and an aesthetically inviting dining room. These modalities were used to tempt the appetite. Nutritious snacks were also available during the day.

Independence was covertly encouraged by the institution by requiring residents on the second floor to be independent with activities of daily living, as well as coming to the dining room for meals, and maintaining their own individual suites. In addition, the theme of independence was encouraged by allowing residents to maintain their own car, and to come and go without restrictions.

The cultural values of privacy were evident in the resident's individual suites. Each person had her own private suite, complete with kitchen and bathroom. Anna's car was a symbol of privacy for her. This was evident in her statement, "I can take a ride in my car when I feel like getting away from the place." This privacy is Anna's display of independence. Her car is a bridge to the world beyond the community residence. The cultural symbol of money was conspicuously evident in the form of a suite with many rooms in a private section of the building, and a personal housekeeper, monopolized by a wealthy couple. This could be connected to independence.

Finally, fellowship was identified by Anna as one of her reasons for coming to live at the residence. It is apparent in the following statements, "I didn't want to live alone. You have someone to talk to. There are always people around. I have lots of friends." During our conversation she described them as "a nice group of friends here." Anna spoke negatively at the lack of male friends, and the fact that most of the male residents were married. The fact that she is concerned about this would indicate that she still considers herself a sexual person. What's interesting here is that there are three moments of age-grading. The issues revolve around health, activity, and independence. Health is important because it maps with activity and independence. Here we have a different approach than the previous talks. This talk has to do with the boundary between the second floor and the third floor. In this instance the markers are clearly set by the boundary. When one crosses over the boundary of the second floor to the third floor, one is probably disabled and will need assistance.

IX

The Dilemma of a Nursing Home Admission

For one thing is certain as we grow older: The few people who
have truly passed through us
And us through them, until the
Dreams, images, memories, are
Past sorting out, these
People become precious links
To our continuity.
(Gail Sheehy, 1976, p. 302).

This interview is with a woman named Jody. It centers on the feelings of an adult child, two weeks after placing her father in a nursing home. The interview took place in a small town in upstate New York.

BACKGROUND INFORMATION

John is an 85 year-old male with Parkinson's disease (a chronic nervous system disease characterized by muscular weakness and gait impairment that is potentially quite debilitating). He is the father of four grown children, two men and two women. All are married and have children, except one son, a physician who lives in a distant state. John had been on anti-Parkinson medicine for several years. Recently he refused to take the medication and had been reported by his wife to be confused and delusional. He started getting up at night and getting dressed, and stating, "I'm going to work." Finally, a decision was made by the family to place him in a nursing home. By Jody's account, it was a catch 22 position. Either her father had to be placed in a nursing home, or her mother would have a nervous breakdown, related to the father's behavior. Her mother was seeing a psychiatrist and is currently on anti-depressant medication. Jody is the youngest of the adult children, and she seems to accept most of the responsibility for her parents. She is married and the mother of three children. She works part-time in a near-by hotel.

The interview took place in Jody's living room. As we spoke, her children played in the backyard sand box. It was a beautiful day in July, the children's voices from the yard denoted a happy and boisterous tone, yet Jody's face portrayed a note of sadness.

FACE TO FACE TALK

The following is a summary of our conversation:

Ethnographer: Hi Jody, how are you?

Jody: OK, I guess. How are things with you?

Ethnographer: Fine, how is the family?

Jody: Willy is fine. The kids are great. Its my parents I'm concerned about. It's like being in a catch 22 situation.

Ethnographer: I'm glad you could talk to me. As I told you on the phone I'm interested in talking to you about your parents, and how their lives impact on you and your family.

Jody: It's been a nightmare if you really want to know.

Ethnographer: That bad!

Jody: Yes! Its been such a dilemma. We recently put my father in a nursing home.

Ethnographer: Oh!

Jody: Well he stopped taking his medicine you know, for his Parkinson's disease. You know he had been on this for a long time.

Ethnographer: Yes! I knew that.

Jody: Well, he was off the wall. Getting up at night, getting dressed, telling my mother he was going to work.

Ethnographer: How did your mother handle this?

Jody: Not very well. I guess his illness had been getting to her for a while. She says she felt closed up in the house, and was afraid of him at night. She's been going to a psychiatrist, and he has her on pills. She said she couldn't deal with it any longer.

Ethnographer: When we spoke before, your father had a woman coming in during day time hours to care for him.

Jody: Yes! And she gave him such good care, but mom said he needed 24-hour care, and the only place for that was a nursing home.

Ethnographer: How did you feel about that?

Jody: Terrible! I hated to see him go to a nursing home, but if he didn't go my mother would have had a nervous breakdown. I thought of bringing him to my house, but with the children and work and all, it wouldn't work.

Ethnographer: How about your brothers and sister?

Jody: Well they couldn't take care of him either. They would help a little, but that wasn't enough.

Ethnographer: How is he adjusting to the nursing home?

Jody: He's not. He looks angry. He spits out the pills. The first couple of days when he got up, they put him in a chair in the corridor and tied him to the chair. They called it restraints.[1] He was seated next to a 98 year old lady who hollers and cries all day. He looks so sad I really want to cry for him.

Ethnographer: I'm sure you feel bad. It must be difficult for him, I'm not surprised he's angry, but I guess they are restraining him for his own protection, so he doesn't fall.

Jody: That's a joke! He was in there less than a week, and he fell and broke his hip. Now he's in the hospital.

Ethnographer: Jody, I'm so sorry!

Jody: Guess what! We have to pay the nursing home a daily rate to hold his bed until he returns.

Ethnographer: A daily rate?

Jody: Yes! Otherwise they can give his bed to someone else, and then they may not have a bed for him when he is ready to return to the nursing home.

Ethnographer: Are the beds that scarce?

Jody: Up here, yes!

Ethnographer: How long will he be in the hospital?

Jody: Possibly another week. Then they will send him back to the nursing home, and he'll have physical therapy there.

Ethnographer: How is he doing now?

Jody: Not too well. They get him out of bed, but he's not too cooperative. I worry about him when he goes back to the nursing home.

Ethnographer: Are you afraid he will fall again?

Jody: Yes! I wonder if their Physical Therapy Department can help him. He has such a long way to go.

UNPLEASANT PROSPECTS

When the father became ill with Parkinson's disease the family hired a full-time practical nurse in the day-time to care for him. At a cost of $500 a week, her services ate up much of the parent's $50,000 savings. As time went on, they replaced the nurse with a home-health aide. While her salary was less, the weekly expenditure continued to exhaust their savings. In time, the family began to fear for their economic survival. Two years after the father's initial diagnosis, the parents savings were depleted. The father's pension and their social security barely covered the expenses of their house, and their grocery and utility bills. The burden of paying for the home-health aide fell on the children. This process continued for over a year, then the father's condition deteriorated. In order to maintain the father in the home, they would need an aide around the clock. At first the children took turns caring for the father, but this placed further stress on the family, and did not meet the mother's needs.

THE DECISION

Finally a decision was made to admit the father to a nursing home that was located a few miles from his home. This would prevent a crisis with the mother, and financially it would be an advantage. John's institutional expenses would be covered by public funds. However, John's fall and subsequent hospitalization after a week of residency in the home changed all that. One must be a resident of the home for 30 days before the state will pay for the room during hospitalization, therefore John did not qualify.

Jody looked pensive as she described the events that took place with her father. He had always been a proud man, rather vain about his appearance. Although he always had clean clothes in his closet, he would insist on wearing the same stained clothes day after day. Shaving and haircuts also created a battle. It hurt to see him unkempt. This man that always had a certain kind of nobility about him.

He had been an avid reader, always paying weekly visits to the library, and subscribing to periodicals such as *National Geographic*. He instilled a love of books in all his children by reading to them, taking them on trips to the library, and most of all, by his example. Jody used to brag that her father could discuss any topic. He was a self-educated man. Now it was painful to watch him just sit in front of the television hour after hour and stare.

CLOSING THE BOUNDARIES

On the day of his admission to the nursing home, her father sat stubbornly on the bed refusing to look at anybody. He pleaded loudly with Jody and the others, "How can you do this to me?" Then his shoulders began to shake as he tried to hold back the tears and sobs. Jody's voice trembled as she described how she wanted to take him to her own home and care for him; but she knew this was an impossible task. "He had devoted his life to taking care of us," she explained, "and I felt like we were abandoning him." Aging and illness had sent a cruel reminder; "I knew I had to face my father's mortality."

Like many other men and women, one could hypothesize that John never expected to spend his final days in a nursing home. While he may have felt strong enough and competent enough to live at home, it was deemed by his family that this was not possible. For John it was a jail sentence. His anger was displayed by his rebellion against the policies of the institution. Unfortunately his actions created a further dilemma.

UNLOCKING THE THEMES

In the discussion just described the interaction created a dialogue of aging that identified the topics of family and money. The concept of the change in the relationship of the family is closely meshed with kinship. Caring, in the mode that someone has to take care of that person, is closely linked with money. The notion of grief, guilt, health, and activity, are also implied and form part of the dialogue. Here, context overwhelmed the event, it became aging in culture shock. It displayed an example of how each age-grade creates its own symbols.

In this interview money was a central issue. It is grounded in the issue of sending the father to a nursing home. If he could afford 24-hour care at home, perhaps the mother would be more amenable to letting him stay at home. Money was addressed in the discussion of paying for the nursing home bed while the father was in the hospital. It was discussed as a benefit vis-a-vis John's residence in the nursing home would be covered by public funds. It was a major family issue when the parent's savings were exhausted and the children had to subsidize the home health-aide. It had to do with care and the relationship between the family. For example, Jody would like to care for her father but she has to work and take care of her family. Her father needs 24-hour care, which costs a lot of money. The only place this can be provided is in a nursing home, subsidized by taxes.

Grief is implied by Jody when she lamented her father's experiences in the nursing home and openly stated, "I feel terrible." It is also evident as she described, "The father that used to be: a reader, a talker, and a man that was meticulous about his appearance." Here grief maps with age-grading, as she described, "Age and illness sending a cruel reminder," and recognizing that she had to face her father's mortality in the imminent future.

Guilt is overtly hurled at Jody by her father when he exclaimed, "How can you do this to me," on his admission to the nursing home.

Jody's response, "I wanted to take care of him," was a mixture of grief and guilt.

The notion of activity is implied in John's getting up at night, and the statement of "I'm going to work." However, the talk suggests its opposite. This is not to say that opposite implies contradiction; however, activity implies independence, and this is connected with being sick. What's bad about being sick is one cannot be independent, yet activity is a state of being in-between. John is still somewhat healthy but not independent. The inference is that he is cognitively impaired. When he went to the nursing home he was restrained, or "tied to the chair," as Jody described it. He moved from the activities of home to the boundaries of restraints in the nursing home. His frame was decided. John's bridge to the outside world has collapsed. According to Bateson (1972), the environment is already there.

One could ask the question, is John in harmony with his environment? Can we make a distinction between language and behavior?

At the end of the preceding inquiry we had some discussion about money and the relationship between the generations. Here we see how this talk gets expanded when one of its possibilities had to be implemented. Aging indeed has to do with money as well as definition, that is, somebody has to take care of that person. This leads to changes in the family that must be talked about: "Who is going to take care of that person?" One major feature of this language is that it is marked as difficult in the statement by Jody, "It is a nightmare." These are the themes. This is the way people talk about aging. While aging does start with birth, in fact all the cultures say so, there is a special age-grade to which this issue addresses. In the following pages, I will discuss the patterns of this language.

NOTES

[1] Currently, most nursing homes have a policy to restrict the use of physical restraints. This concept evolved "When the Restraint-Free Nursing Home Program was launched in 1991." Additionally, the Federal Nursing Home Reform Law of 1987 says that: 1) restraints may be used only if the use is

to insure the physical safety of the resident or other residents. 2) Only upon the written order of a physician that gives the circumstances and time when the restraints may be used (A Guide for Residents and Families).

The Common wealth fund. (1991). *Restraint-free nursing home program.* New York.

Long Term Ombudsman Program, (1987). *A Guide for residents and families.* Denver Regional Council of Governments.

Sheehy, G. (1976). *Passages: Predictable crises of adult life.* New York: P.Dutton & Co. Inc.

X

Patterns of Aging

(Aging) is more a cultural than a normative designation, and it is widely understandable because a variety of somewhat different normative prescriptions may be attributed to it. What is widely shared is likely to be the cultural meaning of the unit, while the norm, fully and properly described is very much more specific, at a narrower degree of generality, more restricted in scope and context, and not widely shared outside of a particular social field. (David M. Schneider, 1976, p. 202)

This chapter will describe the patterns of aging that I heard in the language. Perhaps Schneider's discussion of culture will serve as a starting point.

Each setting produced its own language, albeit at a level relevant to the context in which it took place. While the categories around which this talk was formed were similar, the norm for each setting was different. During each interaction certain issues surfaced. The discourse clustered around themes that framed the interview. These unifying concepts in the cultural vocabulary were the spokes in the wheel that framed the unified whole.

The themes of age language converged around independence. It was a major focus of the talk. Remaining independent was always mentioned. Often it was spoken about explicitly, sometimes implicitly, but it was always there. It was a frame of reference for most issues.

Independence was generally linked to health and money, and was connected to activity. The themes contained family relationships and the language of age-grading. Independence was the key interest and all other interests mapped with it as demonstrated by: (a) John's struggle against his admission to a nursing home, (b) the respondents in the community residence, (c) Anna's car, (d) Priscilla's effort to remain on the second floor, (e) Mrs. Haverty's prescription for staying active, and (f) Mrs. Doyle's modalities for remaining healthy. All represent the categories around which the respondents centered their talk.

In the language of the frail elderly, remaining healthy and staying active are two categories that contribute to independence. That is what most of them seem to talk about. One could inquire why health is so important, and the response would be that it can prevent you from being independent. If you are ill, you cannot be independent because you need someone to take care of you. However, with activity you can be in a state of in-between, where you are still relatively healthy, but cannot really be active because you are not independent.

In pursuing the analysis, you see the flip-side of independence, and this involves family and money. In general, as long as the focus of aging is a personal event, we can talk about the benefits of health, activity, and independence. But when ill-health occurs, then the talk about family and money transpires. John's situation is representative of this side of independence; one can see it involves family and money, and it presented a dilemma to the family. Here money was an issue. If enough money was available, perhaps the family could have hired a full-time aide to care for him, and his admission to the nursing home would not be necessary. The stress of the event caused tension within the family. This was vehemently expressed by Jody.[1]

In the community residence, the rich couple are also an instance of this myth. Here money provided them with ancillary help around the clock. The benefits also included a large comfortable suite and an independent lifestyle. Additionally, in the community residence independence was clearly demarcated by the boundary between the second and third floors previously discussed in the representative setting[2]. If you get sick and cannot use a walker, even though you are mentally alert, your boundaries are decided.

Mrs. Haverty maintained her independence within the confines of her home, yet her environment, in some respect, simulated a nursing home. Her boundaries were defined within the realm of her apartment. Her independence impinged on the support of her family, friends, and her comfortable pension.

Mrs. Doyle maintained her independence within the borders of her apartment and beyond. Presently she is not classified as frail elderly, as she functions independently. She maintained her health by prescriptive medication, diet, and treatment modalities for her hypertension and diabetes respectively. Her boundaries extended beyond her apartment to include the outside world of the senior center, the shopping center, her church, and the homes of her friends and family. She is not confined to an institution or an apartment like the preceding respondents. However, money could be a threat to her independence. She spoke of living on a fixed income, and the prohibitive cost of her medication. The redeeming factor here was that the health care agency she attended accepts her Medicare coverage. Again, the impact of health and money was demonstrated.

In the interview with the group of friends, money talk in the form of taxes led to an argument. There was also the "they talk" regarding money (i.e., " They pay a lot of money for medications"). But who they are was never defined. The issue produced tension that resulted in a fight.

In general, lack of independence does not just denote ill-health or dependence, it also involves the family and money. It is not purely a matter of abstract dependence or impaired health. Aging costs society a lot of money in the form of taxes. When your parents are ill it costs you money, time, and disruption in your life-style; and somehow this seems to be more visible in the language of the frail aging, than the media.

In my analysis of the language, I noticed there is a continuous mention of age-grading. The talk is clearly articulated throughout all of the settings. Even when the group of friends were refuting when aging began. It was clear there was a before and after. There is a moment when you enter a new age-grade. It is evident throughout the data and the media that everybody will talk about the age-grading system. In all the language everywhere there is mention of it, and it is not surprising that it occurred in all the settings. However this language is more complex, because it is quite evident that in the dialogue I heard there are two stages of aging. It may not map with the biology of aging, but certainly in the language that I heard, you have that moment when you go into a home and age-grading is part of the discussion. Age-grading is used functionally but not definitively because nobody will define it.

The concept of the elderly and the stereotypes so celebrated in the literature and other places did not reveal itself in terms of the language or behavior in these settings. What connects these spokes in the wheel is that the patterns are similar. The myth of aging is a myth. Eventually, everybody ages and suffers some loss of independence. The boundary is not attached to a time but to a shift in behavior, and the shift is marked by things like moving to a nursing home. Just which relations are particularly subject to tension, and the form of its expression, has a lot to do with structural aspects that shape patterns of independence and its links with health, money, activity, and family relationships. What may aggravate the tensions is ill-health; this, in turn, creates a severe strain on the family and other identified categories.

This is where independence becomes a key issue; despite poor health and other inadequacies, adequate finances can allay a lot of the strain. It may not buy you health, but it can make the situation more comfortable and facilitate your independence.

These are the patterns of aging that I heard in the language. However Mead (1975) warns us that, "One has always to remember that the pattern one discerns is only one of many that might be worked out through different approaches to the same human situation" (p. 155).

Finally, I would argue that the data I collected did provide some valuable information on the links between the myth of aging and the elderly. It sheds light on the fact that everybody ages; some believe it is by progression like the organization of the settings in this study, others believe it is an individual process.

What is important is that the informants in the study did not fit the stereotypes. Perhaps in some instances the stereotypes were imposed, for example, John in the nursing home. The myth of aging seems to be just that, a myth. Like the poor, the elderly will be always with us.

NOTES

1 This was evident in Jody's talk about her father. The parents' savings were depleted. The burden of paying for a home-health aide fell on the children. The hardship returned, when they had to pay for the father's room in the Nursing Home, while he was in the hospital. It was also the issue that influenced the family's decision to admit him to a nursing home. If he remained at home he would need 24 hour care which the family could not afford.

2 The third floor as defined by the adult community residence is the floor that residents are sent to if they have a stroke or any type of debilitating illness that prevents them from carrying out activities of daily living independently. It emulates a nursing home. I have used it as an analogy in the analysis, since it is a perfect example of a marker that defines the boundaries.

Mead, M. (1975). *Blackberry winter: My earlier years.* New York: Pocket Book Edition.

Schneider, D.M. (1976). Notes toward a theory of culture. In K. Basso, & H. Selby (Eds.), *Meaning in anthropology.* Albuquerque, NM: University of New Mexico Press.

XI
Epilogue: Recurring Threads

In summary, this qualitative study presented a moment in the lives of aging individuals. At the onset of this research I proceeded with the notion that aging is a myth, not folklore or an illusion. Aging is a myth of cultural stereotypes that reflects our talk of elderly individuals. It is part of the legacy of growing old in American society. A major goal of the research was to identify the markers that demarcate the boundaries of aging.

Initially, I became aware of this quandary through my work as a staff nurse, and later in my role as a nursing instructor. I noticed many diagnoses, prognoses, and care were obscured by the label of aging. Another issue was discharge planning; it seemed the initial discharge plan of most elderly patients included some consideration of transfer to a nursing home. Yet, when one worked with elderly people on a one-on-one basis, the true potential of the individual surfaced, not the reflection of the stereotype.

The situation sparked my interest. I was curious about the structure and form of the language. I spoke to patients, professional peers, relatives, and friends. In addition, I looked at elderly people in the community and viewed the media for comparison. To carry out my research, I spent a year-and-a-half in the community conducting an ethnography. I selected settings where I could talk to elderly people. I wanted to see how the elderly themselves spoke about aging. In contrast, I wanted to hear how an average group of friends would discuss aging. I wondered if the stereotypes really did fit someone growing old in America. My question became one that involved intergenerational difference, involving stereotypes, and patterns of aging.

The age range of my elderly respondents was from 75 to 92 years. Many in this age group are classified as frail elderly in medical and gerontological circles. The language that I heard portrayed interested people, trying to maintain their independence in the world against many odds. One respondent had limitations in ambulation, another had a chronic metabolic disorder, as well as living on a modest pension. They maintained their independence by keeping healthy, staying active, and living within the guidelines of a therapeutic health regime, often by simplistic, rudimentary methods, yet always attempting to maintain their dignity. Some respondents maintained their independence by assistance from family and friends.

What is interesting is these elderly people did not fit the cultural construct of aging, nor did they want to be classified as old. The talk gave testimony to this concept. The findings indicated that independence is the main issue, and it is closely connected to health and activity. When elderly people maintain their health and independence, life is generally smooth. Those were the markers that defined the boundaries in the respective settings that I visited. What upsets their world is ill-health, which places their independence in jeopardy. Impaired health inevitably puts a strain on their financial resources, and on the family or significant other.

The epitome of this talk is evident in the account of one elderly individual's admission to a nursing home. The person in question was John, an 85 year-old male with Parkinson's disease. The decision to admit him was made by his family; it was influenced by the disruption John caused at home, and the family's financial inability to continue to hire a home-health-aide on a 24-hour basis. In essence, we have family need influenced by money and baptized by the culture.

John's new boundaries included imposed restraints to a chair to prevent him from falling. He rebelled against these limitations and subsequently fell and broke his hip. One could ask, were these boundaries artificially created or was it the patient's fault? Or does this episode map with my initial hypothesis about institutional labeling and a reflective approach to patient care. The literature attests to this. "The question of what one is, is not only a matter of one's own choice, but the label of others as well" (Daniel Bell, Ethnicity and Social Change, p. 159). Was this episode similar to the tailor, and the lady with Paget's Disease, discussed earlier in "Reasons for the Study." I refer the reader back to the stories in the introductory chapter. Is this the way to create a boundary? Varenne (1977) writes, "Analyzing ritual and symbolic behavior does not necessarily reveal the specific 'needs' of the participants" (p. 166).

It would seem that in the institutional setting the stage is set, one cannot transcend culture. Is the central dynamic money in the form of employing more health care staff? Does this also relate to the family? As a nurse I say this with trepidation. My intent is not to critique institutional care, but to analyze the language. Suffice it to say that independence is meshed with the variables of health and activity. They complement one another; if one's health is impaired you probably lose your independence, and in turn, your activity will be curtailed. This concept was also evident in the second floor-third floor boundaries of the adult residence setting. However, money is an asset. This concept was inferred in the description of the rich couple in this residence. Adequate financial resources can make the situation easier, and in some way maintain the individual's independence.

When people talk about aging, their own personal aging talk evolves; when they talk in general, or in the media, you get the extremes. I began with the notion that there existed a cultural construct of aging. What I found was a group of people who sometimes do aging, and at other times, do something else. What is important is that it tends to be a ritual; the pattern is essentially a pattern that is part of the sorting process. It seems that on one hand, elderly people are doing what other people do, and are accepted and integrated into society. While on the other hand, they are often ostracized, even by their own age group, both physically and socially. Thus, there seems to be some degree of contradiction existing in the culture. Contrary to earlier negative stereotypes of aging, the respondents in this study were a diverse group of people, possessing a wide range of characteristics common to all individuals.

Finally, none of the respondents could define the term aging. It seems the elderly respondents rejected the stereotypes. One claimed:

"I'm not one of them; "another remarked, "I have blood pressure as good as a young woman's."

This is what I see as a major value of the study! Looking at communication on aging within the settings has given attention, I hope, to the complex cultural world of the elderly. It presented a moment in their lives, and this I hope is reflective of what aging people do in any other social context in America. While I recognize that all people age, and this is communicated in the data, it is not accomplished by a precise set of norms and stereotypes at a designated age. Yet this is the implicit message of the myth. To recapitulate, stereotypes, norms, and designated age-grades are the markers of the myth. This message, in turn, probably impacts negatively on the elderly, and in some situations, impedes their health care.

Before concluding, I will identify areas for future research. The nurse is a central figure in dealing with individuals and their families in the institutional setting, the community, and in her everyday dealings with individuals. However, her participation in co-constructing the myths of aging has not been documented. I presume this would be a fertile area of research. Being a Registered Nurse myself, I believe this study gave me an entirely new way of assessing elderly people and patients in general. Another area for study would be the family, perhaps a study dealing with the way family members participate unwittingly in assisting elderly members of their family to do aging. Finally, I posit, an interesting thesis would be, children's perception of aging in society.

In this research, I have tried to share a slice of the culture of aging, the language, the myths, and so on. Have I achieved what I started out to do; have I analyzed the circumstances appropriately? This is a mote question, as Varenne (1977) writes:

> Levi-Strauss has emphasized many times, no analysis of human phenomena can ever be finished and closed. Life goes on, and continually offers new material that could modify the analysis as it was left dangling, collecting the odds and ends of phenomena that he encountered during his fieldwork. (p. 10)

Perhaps the questions for future research, if implemented, will give a different perspective, and will further society's comprehension of the aging and who they are.

NOTES

Bell, D. (1975). Ethnicity and social change. *In Ethnicity: Theory and experience.* Cambridge, Massachusetts: Harvard University Press.

Varenne, H. (1977). *American's together: Structured diversity in a midwestern town,* New York Teachers College Press.

Glossary

Age-grading Arranging individuals in a status according to age.

Animal fats Saturated fats derived from animal foods; such as egg yolks, beef and liver.

Biopsychosocial A holistic approach to patient care that includes the biological, psychological and social needs of the individual.

Blood sugar Level of glucose in the blood; normally a range of 60 to 100mg/100ml of blood.

Cardiovascular Pertaining to the heart and blood vessels.

Cerebral arteriosclerosis A disease of the arterial blood vessels in the brain characterized by thickening, hardening and loss of elasticity in the walls of the vessel.

Crockpot Very slow cooking electric pot.

Communion Sacramental host in the Catholic religion.

Diabetes Mellitus Chronic disorder of carbohydrate metabolism, characterized by elevated blood glucose; resulting from inadequate production and utilization of insulin.

Delusion A false fixed belief despite the absence of specific evidence.

Glucometer A device used to measure blood glucose; using a few drops of blood from the individual's finger.

Insulin A hormone secreted by the pancreas to promote the metabolism of blood glucose and to maintain the normal blood glucose level. Exogenous, synthetic insulin is injected by diabetics to achieve these goals.

Kinesic movement Gestures that convey meaning in a particular context.

Mature diabetic An individual with adult onset diabetes sometimes called type 11, who may require oral anti- diabetic agents or insulin therapy and diet for the condition.

Medicare Federally sponsored health insurance for individuals over sixty-five years old. There are two parts to the program, hospital insurance, and voluntary supplementary medical insurance.

Medicare assignment The amount Medicare approves for a specific medical service or supply. If a physician accepts the assignment he will not charge the patient more than the sanctioned amount.

Older Americans Act   Evolved from legislation enacted in 1965 to provide community based social service for older adults, and amended in 1973 to establish local units .

Proxemic level of communication   Space claimed by an individual through body language.

Psychomotor skills   Tasks requiring physical activity in concert with cognitive process.

Qualitative Research   A nonnumerical method of obtaining data through interviews, Participant observation and document analysis.

Restraints (In medicine)   A device, such as a wristlet or body vest; used to limit movement or immobilize a patient to promote his safety.

Tripod cane   A cane with three prongs or legs that provides a wide base of support for an individual with poor balance.

Walker   A lightweight tubular frame used to assist a person in ambulating.

Bibliography

Amoss, P. & Harrell, S. (Eds.), *Other Ways of Growing Old*. Stanford, Ca: Stanford University Press, 1981.

Atchley, R. A. *Continuity Theory of Normal Aging*. The Gerontologist, 29:2, 183-190, 1989.

Atchley, R.C. (Ed.), *The Sociology of Retirement*. New York: John Wiley & Sons, 1960.

Bakhtin, M.M. *The Dialogic Imagination*. Austin, Texas: University of Texas Press, 1986.

Bakhtin, M.M. *Problems of Dostoevsky's Poetics*. Minneapolis: University of Minnesota Press, 1984.

Basso, K., & Selby, H. (Eds.), *Meaning in Anthropology*. Albuquerque, New Mexico: University of New Mexico Press, 1976.

Bateson, G. *Steps to an Ecology of Mind*. New York: Ballantine Books, 1972.

Bateson, G., & Bateson, M.C. *Angels Fear: Towards an Epistemology of the Sacred*. New York: Macmillan Publishing Company, 1987.

Beck, C.K., & Shue, V.M. *Alzheimer's Disease: Where Small Victories Create Large Hopes*. Sigma Theta Tau International. Reflections, first quarter, 11-12, 1997.

Benedict, Ruth. *Patterns of Culture*. Boston: Houghton Mifflin Company, 1961.

Binstock, R.H. & Shanas, E. (Eds.), *Handbook of Aging and the Social Sciences*. New York: Van Nostrand and Reinhold Company, 1976.

Birdwhistell, R.L. *Kinetics and Context*. Philadelphia: University of Pennsylvania Press, 1970.

Borgotta, E.F., & McCluskey, N.G. (Eds.), *Aging and Society*. Beverly Hills, California: Sage Publications Inc. 1980

Briggs, C.L. *Learning How to Ask: A Sociolinguistic Appraisal of the Role of the Interview in Social Science Research*. Cambridge, New York: Cambridge University Press, 1986.

Butler, R.N. *Don't Just Cut Medicare: Let's Fix It*. Geriatrics: Medicine for Mid-life and Beyond, 50:9, 11-12, 1995.

Carrithers, M., Collins, S., and Lukes, S. *The Category of the Person: Anthropology, Philosophy, History*. Cambridge University Press, 1985.

Cavan, R.S., Burgess, E.W., Havinghurst, R.J., & Goldhamer, H. *Personal Adjustment in Old Age*. Chicago: Science Research Associates, 1949.

Chudacoff, H.P. *How Old are Your? Age Consciousness in American Culture*. Princeton, New Jersey: Princeton University Press, 1989.

Clark K., & Holquist M. *Mikhail Bakhtin* Cambridge, Massachusetts: The Belknap Press of Howard University Press, 1984.

Coberg, A., Lynch, D., & Mauretish, B. *Harnessing Ideas to Release Restraints*. Geriatric Nursing, 12:3, 133-134, 1991.

Cumming, E., & Henry, W.E. *Growing Old: The Process of Disengagement*. New York: Basic Books, 1961.

Decker, D.L., (Ed.), *Social Gerontology*, Boston: Little Brown & Company, 1980.

Evans, L. & Strumpf, N. *Freeing the Ties that Bind*. Sigma Theta Tau International, Reflections, third quarter, 8-10, 1996.

Foner, N. *Ages in Conflict: A Cross Cultural Perspective on Inequality Between Old and Young*. New York: Columbia University Press, 1984.

Foreman, M.D. & Zane, D. *Nursing Strategies for Acute Confusion in Elders*. American Journal of Nursing, 4: 44-52, 1996.

Frake, C.O. *Language and Cultural Description*. Stanford, California: Stanford University Press, 1980.

Friedan, B. *Not for Women Only*. Modern Maturity, April-May, 66-71, 1989.

Fry, C.L. (Eds.), Dimensions: Aging, Culture, and Health. New York: J.F. Bergin Publishers Inc. 1981.

Galsworthy, T.D., & Wilson, P.L. *Osteoporosis: It Steals More Than Bone*. American Journal of Nursing, 6:27-34, 1996.

Gardner, H. *The Quest for Mind: Piaget, Levi-Strauss, and the Structuralist Movement*, New York: Vintage Books, 1974.

Geertz, C. *The Interpretation of Cultures*. New York: Basic Books, Inc. 1973.

Glazer, N., & Moynihan, D.P. *Ethnicity: Theory and Experience*. Massachusetts: Harvard University Press, 1975.

Goffman, E. *Behavior in Public Places: Notes on the Social Organization of Gatherings*. The Free Press: division of Macmillan Publishing Company, 1963.

Goffman, E. *Interaction Ritual: Essays on Face to Face Behavior*. New York: Pantheon Books, 1967.

Goffman, E. *Forms of Talk*. Philadelphia: University of Pennsylvania Press, 1981.

Harris, L. & Associates, Inc. *The Myth and Reality of Aging in America.* Washington, D.C.: The National Council on Aging, 1975.

Heath, S.B. *Ways with Words: Language, Life and Working Communities and Classrooms.* Cambridge, New York: Cambridge University Press, 1983.

Houston, K. & Lach, H., *Restraints: How do you Score?* Geriatric Nursing, 11, 5: 231-232, 1991.

Kelly, G.A. *The Catholic Marriage Manual.* New York: Random House, 1958.

Kilpatrick, M.K., Ford, S., & Castelloe, B.P. *Storytelling: An Approach to Client Centered Care.* Nurse Educator, 22, No. 2:38-40, March/April, 1997.

Kolanowski, A.M., & Whall, A.L. *Life Span Perspective of Personality in Dementia.* Image: Journal of Nursing Scholarship. 28:4, 102-106, Winter, 1996.

McDermott, R.P., & Hood, L. *Children In and Out of School.* Washington, D.C.: Center for Applied Linguistics, 1982.

Mead, M. *Blackberry Winter: My Earlier Years.* New York: Pocket Book Edition, 1975.

Needham, J.F. *Gerontological Nursing: a Restorative Approach.* Albany, New York: Delmar Publishers Inc, 1993.

Neugarten, B.L. (Ed.), *Personality in Middle and Late Life.* New York: Atherson.

Pasquali, E.A., Arnold, H.M., and DeBasio, N. *Mental Health Nursing* (3rd ed.) St. Louis: The C.V. Mosby Company, 1989.

Peterson, B. *The Mind Body Connection.* The Canadian Nurse, 92, 1:29-31, 1996.

Pietrukowicz, M. & Johnson, M., *Using Life Histories to Individualize Nursing Home Staff Attitudes Toward Residents.* The Gerontologist, 31, 1: 102-106, 1991.

Platt, D.W. *Long Engagements.* Stanford, California: Stanford University Press, 1980.

Riley, M.M., Johnson, M., & Foner, A. *Aging and Society.* Vol. 3, A Sociology of Age Stratification, New York: Russell Sage, 1972.

Robb, S.S. Resources in the environment of the aged. In A.G. Yurick, S.S. Robb, B.E. Spier, & N.J. Ebert (Eds.), *The Aged Person and the Nursing Process.* New York: Appleton-Century-Crofts, 1980.

Rose, A., & Peterson, W. *Older People and Their Social World: The Subculture of Aging.* Philadelphia: F.A. Davis.

Rossoc, I. *Socialization to Old Age*. Berkley, California: University of California Press, 1974.

Scheflen, A.E., & Ashcraft, N. *Human Territories: How We Behave in Space Time*. Englewood Cliffs, New Jersey: Prentice Hall, Inc.

Schieffelin, B.B., and Ochs, E. *Language Socialization Across Cultures*. Cambridge: Cambridge University Press, 1986.

Schultz, A. Common Sense and Scientific Interpretations of Human Action. In H. Garfinkel (Ed.), *Studies in Ethnomethodology*. New York: Prentice Hall, Inc. 1959.

Schultz, A. Rules as Explanations of Action. In D.L. Wieder (Ed.), *Language and Social Reality*. The Hague, Netherlands: Mouton and Co. 1962.

Sheehy, G. Passages: *Predictable Crisis of Adult Life*. New York: P. Dutton & Co. Inc. 1976.

Sheehy, G. *The Silent Passage: Menopause*. New York: G. Merritt Corporation, Random House. 1991, 1992.

Stanley, M., Beare, P.G. *Gerontological Nursing*. Philadelphia, F.A. Davis Co. 1995.

Stocker, S. *Six Tips for Caring For Aging Parents*. American Journal of Nursing, 9:32-33, 1996.

Thomas, J. *Predictors of Satisfaction with Children's Help for Younger and Older Elderly Parents*. Journal of Gerontology: Social Sciences. 43, 1:9-14, 1988.

Varenne, H. *Americans Together: Structured Diversity in a Midwestern Town*. New York: Teachers College Press, 1977.

Varenne, H. *American School Language: Culturally Patterned Conflicts in a Suburban High School*. New York: Irvington Publishers, Inc. 1983.

Varenne, H. *Symbolizing America*. Lincoln: London University of Nebraska Press, 1986.

Webster, J.A. *Key to Healthy Aging: Exercise*. Journal of Gerontological Nursing. 14, 12: 9-15, 1988.

Wilson, H.S. *Introducing Research in Nursing*. (2nd ed.) California: Addison-Wesley Nursing, 1993.

Yurick, A.G., Robb, S.S., B.E. Spier & N.J. Ebert (Eds.), *The Aged Person and the Nursing Process*. New York: Appleton-Century-Crofts, 1975.

Zarit, S. H. (Ed.), *Readings in Aging and Death: Contemporary Perspectives*. (2nd ed.) New York: Harper & Row Publishers, 1982.

Index